How To Use This Study Guide

This ten-lesson study guide corresponds to *"What To Do if Answers to Your Prayers Are Delayed or Hindered" With Rick Renner* (Renner TV). Each lesson in this study guide covers a topic that is addressed during the program series, with questions and references supplied to draw you deeper into your own private study of the Scriptures on this subject.

To derive the most benefit from this study guide, consider the following:

First, watch or listen to the program prior to working through the corresponding lesson in this guide. (Programs can also be viewed at **renner.org** by clicking on the Media/Archives links or on our Renner Ministries YouTube channel.)

Second, take the time to look up the scriptures included in each lesson. Prayerfully consider their application to your own life.

Third, use a journal or notebook to make note of your answers to each lesson's Study Questions and Practical Application challenges.

Fourth, invest specific time in prayer and in the Word of God to consult with the Holy Spirit. Write down the scriptures or insights He reveals to you.

Finally, take action! Whatever the Lord tells you to do according to His Word, do it.

For added insights on this subject, it is recommended that you obtain Rick Renner's books *How To Receive Answers From Heaven: What To Do When Your Prayers Go Unanswered* and *Igniting a Powerful Prayer Life: A Sparkling Gems From the Greek Guided Devotional Journal.* You may also select from Rick's other available resources by placing your order at **renner.org** or by calling 1-800-742-5593.

LESSON 1

TOPIC

Praying Inconsistently Can Hinder Prayers From Being Answered

SCRIPTURES

1. **Matthew 5:45** — That ye may be the children of your Father which is in heaven: for he maketh his sun to rise on the evil and on the good, and sendeth rain on the just and on the unjust.
2. **James 1:6** — But let him ask in faith, nothing wavering. For he that wavereth is like a wave of the sea driven with the wind and tossed.

GREEK WORDS

1. "ask" — αἰτέω (*aiteo*): to ask, demand, petition, or to request; pictures one who asks with the full expectation of receiving what was firmly requested
2. "in" — ἐν (*en*): in, inside, located inside, and it gives the impression of this sphere in which this expectant asking is to take place; means being rooted in or from a position of being in faith; James uses this preposition ἐν (*en*) to focus his audience on the starting point for all successful prayer — faith
3. "faith" — πίστις (*pistis*): from πείθω (*peitho*), which pictures one who possesses a rock-solid belief, an absolute confidence, an unmovable conviction, or an unwavering confidence; thus, faith is not up and down one day, back and forth the next day, or indecisive, but is a rock-solid, unwavering force
4. "wavering" — διακρινόμενος (*diakrinomenos*): habitual vacillation; the image of one who goes back and forth and who habitually changes his mind or his faith position
5. "wave" — κλύδων (*kludon*): pictures one wave after another wave or a succession of rising and falling waves
6. "driven with the wind" — ἀνεμίζω (*anemidzo*): derived from ἄνεμος (*anemos*), which depicts fierce winds or turbulence that has the potential to wreak havoc and destruction

A Note From Rick Renner

I am on a personal quest to see a "revival of the Bible" so people can establish their lives on a firm foundation that will stand strong and endure the test as end-time storm winds begin to intensify.

In order to experience a revival of the Bible in your personal life, it is important to take time each day to read, receive, and apply its truths to your life. James tells us that if we will continue in the perfect law of liberty — refusing to be forgetful hearers, but determined to be doers — we will be blessed in our ways. As you watch or listen to the programs in this series and work through this corresponding study guide, I trust you will search the Scriptures and allow the Holy Spirit to help you hear something new from God's Word that applies specifically to your life. I encourage you to be a doer of the Word He reveals to you. Whatever the cost, I assure you — it will be worth it.

> Thy words were found, and I did eat them;
> and thy word was unto me the joy and rejoicing of mine heart:
> for I am called by thy name, O Lord God of hosts.
> — Jeremiah 15:16

Your brother and friend in Jesus Christ,

Rick Renner

Unless otherwise indicated, all scripture quotations are taken from the *King James Version* of the Bible.

Scripture quotations marked (*AMPC*) are taken from the *Amplified® Bible, Classic Edition*. Copyright © 1954, 1958, 1962, 1964, 1965, 1987 by The Lockman Foundation. Used by permission. **www.Lockman.org**.

Scripture quotations marked (*NLT*) are taken from the Holy Bible, *New Living Translation*, copyright © 1996, 2004, 2015 by Tyndale House Foundation. Used by permission of Tyndale House Publishers, Inc., Carol Stream, Illinois 60188. All rights reserved.

Scripture quotations marked (*RIV*) are taken from *Renner Interpretive Version*. Copyright © 2021 by Rick Renner.

What To Do if Answers to Your Prayers Are Delayed or Hindered

Copyright © 2024 by Rick Renner
1814 W. Tacoma St.
Broken Arrow, OK 74012-1406

Published by Rick Renner Ministries
www.renner.org

ISBN 13: 978-1-6675-0983-9

eBook ISBN 13: 978-1-6675-0984-6

All rights reserved. No portion of this book may be reproduced or transmitted in any form or by any means — electronic, mechanical, photocopy, recording, scanning, or other — except for brief quotations in critical reviews or articles, without the prior written permission of the Publisher.

7. "tossed" — ῥιπίζω (*rhipidzo*): raging currents of the sea, but also pictures a dangerous undercurrent; scholars suggest this is the source for the word riptide, which is a dangerous undercurrent caused by atmospheric disturbances that has the potential to drag people into an inescapable undertow where they drown after being carried far away from safety

SYNOPSIS

More than likely, you have been in a situation where you prayed for something but the answers to your prayers were either delayed or never received. What causes these hindrances and delays in our life? This subject is what we will be covering in this series.

The ten lessons in this study titled *What To Do if Answers to Your Prayers Are Delayed or Hindered* will focus on the following topics:

- **Praying Inconsistently** Can Hinder Prayers From Being Answered
- **Praying Incorrectly** Can Hinder Prayers From Being Answered
- **A Lack of Faith** Can Hinder Prayers From Being Answered
- **A Negative Confession** Can Hinder Prayers From Being Answered
- **Bad Relationships** Can Hinder Prayers From Being Answered
- **Spiritual Opposition** Can Hinder Prayers From Being Answered
- **Timing** Can Hinder Prayers From Being Answered
- **Sin** May Affect Your Prayers Being Answered
- What To Do if Answers to Your Prayers Are Delayed or Hindered, Part 1
- What To Do if Answers to Your Prayers Are Delayed or Hindered, Part 2

The emphasis of this lesson:

Faith is the starting point of all prayer. God wants us to boldly ask Him for what we need and to have complete confidence, without wavering or vacillating, that He will answer our prayers. Instead of moving on from what you're believing for, hold on in faith and trust God.

8 Factors That Affect Our Prayers

As we begin this series, it is imperative for you to know that God wants to answer everyone's prayers. This includes those who are saved and those who are unsaved — the just and the unjust. Jesus confirms this in Matthew 5:45 which says:

> **That ye may be the children of your Father which is in heaven: for he maketh his sun to rise on the evil and on the good, and sendeth rain on the just and on the unjust.**

Now, while God certainly wants to bless and take care of everyone, there are certain conditions that can cause our prayers to be hindered or the answers delayed in coming to us. In this study, we are going to examine 8 specific factors that affect our requests to God, including:

1) Praying Inconsistently
2) Praying Incorrectly
3) A Lack of Faith
4) A Negative Confession
5) Bad Relationships
6) Spiritual Opposition
7) Timing
8) Sin

For the remainder of this lesson, we will focus our attention on the obstacle of *praying inconsistently*.

We Are to 'Ask'

Writing under the inspiration of the Holy Spirit, James tells us clearly how we must pray:

> **But let him ask in faith, nothing wavering. For he that wavereth is like a wave of the sea driven with the wind and tossed.**
> —**James 1:6**

One of the first things we can see from James' writing is that it is perfectly okay for us to ask God for the things we need. The word "ask" in this verse is a form of the Greek word *aiteo*, which means *to ask, demand, petition,* or *request*. It is the picture of one who asks with the full expectation of receiving what was firmly requested.

Now, if we look at James 1:5, we see that James has already stated that God answers *generously, abundantly, plentifully, profusely, bountifully*, and *open-handedly* to anyone who humbles himself and asks for His help. Moreover, God's answer is *something provided copiously, amply, extravagantly*, or *lavishly*. But His requirement is that the one asking must ask with a full expectation of receiving what has been requested.

Thus, the person that James is describing does not depict someone who makes requests to God with a *hope-so* attitude, but one who has a firm and full expectation that God will indeed answer.

'In Faith'

Also notice the word "in" from verse 6. It is the little Greek preposition *en*, and it means *in, inside*, or *located inside*. This term gives the impression of the sphere in which this expectant asking is to take place. It means *being rooted in* or *from a position of being in faith*. James uses this preposition *en* to focus his audience on the starting point for all successful prayer — faith.

This is not faith in a general sense but depicts a faith that is solidly rooted in God's Word. A person praying can either pray in the sphere of mountain-moving faith or pray wrongly from a negative viewpoint about the circumstances assailing him.

The one praying in mountain-moving faith fixates his perspective on God's unstoppable ability, and this approach sends doubt into retreat. In contrast, the second person regretfully magnifies his felt opposition to the point of absurdity.

The right place from which to pray is in *faith*, and the word "faith" here is a form of the Greek word *pistis*, which is from the word *peitho*. It pictures *one who possesses a rock-solid belief, an absolute confidence, an unmovable conviction, or an unwavering confidence*. Thus, faith is not up and down one day, back and forth the next day, or indecisive, but is a rock-solid, unwavering force.

'Without Wavering'

James then qualifies the condition of our asking, saying it is to be *without wavering*. The word "wavering" is a translation of the Greek word *diakrinomenos*, which describes *habitual vacillation*. This term depicts the image of one who goes back and forth and who habitually changes his mind or his faith position.

Essentially, James is telling us that a person who is on-again, off-again, and who habitually flip-flops in what he asks, believes, or prays, is not a person who is asking or acting in faith. Instead, real faith continues moving forcefully forward to grab hold of what it believes, and it doesn't flip-flop back and forth in what it asks or believes.

James then proceeds to provide an example of what faith is *not* like, by stating that faith does not act "like a wave of the sea, driven with the wind and tossed." He uses the word *diakrinomenos* — translated here as "wavering" — to give the imagery of tossing waves to convey vacillation in prayer.

Think about the action of waves in the sea. This word "wave," a form of the Greek word *kludon*, pictures one wave after another wave, or a succession of rising and falling waves. If you look out over the sea, waves are always rising and falling, and as each wave forms, they look so impressive. They build and build and build until finally, *bam!* They break and tumble back into the sea, and a new wave is produced.

However, it is not really a new wave; it is just the old wave that has been recycled. It's the same water churned up to make a new wave, and that is what happens again and again and again. It peaks and falls, peaks and falls, peaks and falls. So, while this wave may seem impressive, it never lasts very long because it just tumbles back down into the sea.

"Wavering" faith is a picture of *indecision*.

Imagine a person praying and saying, "God, I know what I want. I want you to do (*fill in the blank*), and I really believe You can do it." But then he changes his mind or flip-flops on what he is believing. His faith is like *a wave on the sea* that builds but then tumbles back down and dissipates into indecision. He is not sure of what he wants.

So this person refocuses on what he desires and begins to pray again. His faith starts rising, and his prayers sound so powerful. But then something negative happens, and he wavers, saying things like, "I'm not really sure if that's what I want or even if God will do it." Again, his faith gives way to indecision. Like the wave, he tumbles back down into the sea, flip-flopping, changing, rising and falling all the time.

James says real faith does not behave like that. Real faith stands for what it believes and does not waver. It remains steadfast and strong — firmly trusting in God and expecting whatever it desires to come to pass.

What Does It Mean To Be 'Driven with the Wind' and 'Tossed'?

What causes wave action? That's right — *wind*. James says that wavering faith is "driven with the wind and tossed" (*see* James 1:6). The phrase "driven with the wind" is translated from the Greek word *anemidzo*, which is derived from *anemos*, and depicts *fierce winds or turbulence that has the potential to wreak havoc and destruction*. The use of this word here tells us that a person whose faith is "driven with the wind" is *one who has the potential of experiencing fierce turbulence, havoc, and destruction in his life*.

This brings us to the word "tossed" — a form of the Greek word *rhipidzo*. It describes *raging currents of the sea* and also pictures *a dangerous undercurrent*. Interestingly, scholars suggest this is the source for the word *riptide*, which is a dangerous undercurrent caused by atmospheric disturbances that has the potential to drag people into an inescapable undertow where they drown after being carried far away from safety.

Essentially, James is letting us know that spiritually immature individuals — those who are easily moved by what they hear and see — are those who habitually vacillate back and forth in what they say or believe. These people suffer the threat of being dragged into a state of spiritual bedlam that has the potential to "drown" them.

Such individuals may not realize the seriousness of indecision, but such habitual wavering back and forth and vacillating in faith — or living in a constant state of indecision — if not halted, can, like a riptide, pull them into an undertow that is difficult to break free from. Hence, one who vacillates must see their actions as a damaging behavior that must be stopped before they are sucked into a constant sea of indecision.

Faith Stands Still and Trusts God

Again, God wants to bless everyone — *including you!* But to receive His blessings, you must operate in faith and not be constantly wavering. *Faith stands still.* It is not constantly changing its mind, flipping back and forth on what it believes.

Oftentimes, God sends the answer, but when the answer arrives, the person who is wavering in faith has already changed his mind and moved on to believe something different. It's as if God's answer shows up at the right address — the address of faith — but the person is no longer living at that address. He has moved on.

When God hears that person pray again, and their faith is rising, He sends the answer. But when the answer shows up, the person is gone once again.

An individual with wavering faith is constantly "changing his address," never standing still in faith on what God has said. Instead, he is constantly flipping back and forth in a state of indecision. James says it is impossible for this person to receive an answer to his prayer (*see* James 1:7).

When we factor in the original Greek meaning of the key words in James 1:6, this is how it reads in the *Renner Interpretive Version* (*RIV*):

> **But this next point is important, so pay close attention. Whoever is asking must do it with an expectation that God really will answer him. In other words, he must ask while being rooted in faith (with unwavering confidence). The one who doesn't stick with it, but who habitually changes his mind — who is up one day and down the next, flip-flopping and going back and forth, "all over the place," in what he asks or believes — is a lot like the waves of the sea. Just as waves rise, fall, and tumble back into the sea over and over, a doubting person is one who keeps changing his mind again and again. He appears to be making progress, but then, suddenly, he changes his mind again and tumbles back into indecision. He is up and down, back and forth, indecisive, and unstable. And as the waves of the sea are endlessly tossed by ferocious winds, one who doubts is thrown here, there, and all around. A person who can't make his mind up about what he asks and believes doesn't realize the dangerous predicament he's in — for like a dangerous riptide,**

his doubt and wavering can pull him perpetually into a sea of indecision.

Rock-Solid Faith Is Built on God's Word

The only way we can remain stable, still, and unwavering is to know what the Word of God says. The Word of God is our anchor, and when we continue in the Word, our faith is fed and strengthened. For example, if we are believing and asking God to heal us, we need to meditate on passages of Scripture that help us know beyond a shadow of a doubt that it is God's will to heal us.

First Peter 2:24 says that by Jesus' stripes — the brutal beating He received on His body — we were healed. When we stand on that promise and speak it out loud over our lives, against the enemy, and to the Lord in prayer, and we refuse to move from that truth, we are *in faith*. It's a decision that results from getting our mind renewed with the truth rather than just developing determination on willpower alone. Once we know the truth, we have to lock in on it.

Friend, God will respond to your prayers when you ask in faith. If you are flip-flopping back and forth all the time, vacillating on what you believe and what you want God to do, your prayers are not going to get answered. That is wind-driven, wind-tossed faith that is like the waves on the sea. To those who operate in this kind of faith, the Bible says, "…Let not that man think that he shall receive any thing of the Lord" (James 1:7).

If you want God's answer to come to you and you want to be blessed, you have to pray in the realm of mountain-moving faith. Again, that word "faith" is the Greek word *pistis*, derived from *peitho*, and it describes *a rock-solid confidence where you are convinced to your core*. That is what God wants for your life. Instead of being a moving target that keeps vacillating back and forth, He wants you to stay in and pray from a place of faith.

Remember, faith stands still. It is confident, determined, rock-solid, and knows what it wants. Faith will not settle for anything less than God's best. It believes God's promises until it receives God's promises.

STUDY QUESTIONS

> Study to shew thyself approved unto God, a workman that
> needeth not to be ashamed, rightly dividing the word of truth.
> — 2 Timothy 2:15

1. The very first step in receiving answers from God to your prayers is to *ask*. Did you know that Jesus urges you to ask for things in prayer? For a fresh perspective on the importance of praying and asking God for what you need, check out what Jesus said in these passages:
   - Matthew 7:7-11
   - Luke 11:9-13
   - John 14:13,14
   - John 15:7

2. Do you tend to vacillate when you pray, going back and forth between confidently trusting and doubting God? Many people do. To help you overcome this indecision, take time now — and whenever doubt arises — to meditate on these verses declaring the faithfulness of God and what He says in His Word:
   - Deuteronomy 7:9 and Lamentations 3:22,23
   - Numbers 23:19 and Hebrews 6:18
   - First Kings 8:56; Psalm 111:7; and Hebrews 10:23
   - First Corinthians 1:9 and Second Thessalonians 3:3

PRACTICAL APPLICATION

> But be ye doers of the word, and not hearers only,
> deceiving your own selves.
> — James 1:22

1. To pray in mountain-moving faith, we must fix our perspective on God's unstoppable ability, not on the opposition or problems we face. Be honest: on what are you focusing as you pray for God's help in your current challenge(s)? Take time to reflect on the instructions found in Hebrews 12:1-3 and Psalm 34:1-3 and hit refresh on your focus.

2. To rekindle faith and hope that God will once again come through for you, recall to memory some of the marvelous ways the Master has helped you in the past — ways in which He protected you, provided for you, had mercy on you, and empowered you with His grace (*see* Psalm 77:11,12.) How does remembering His faithfulness in the past encourage you to trust Him with your present and future?

LESSON 2

TOPIC

Praying Incorrectly Can Hinder Prayers From Being Answered

SCRIPTURES

1. **Matthew 5:45** — That ye may be the children of your Father which is in heaven: for he maketh his sun to rise on the evil and on the good, and sendeth rain on the just and on the unjust.
2. **James 4:3** — Ye ask, and receive not, because ye ask amiss, that ye may consume it upon your lusts.
3. **1 John 5:14,15** — And this is the confidence that we have in him, that, if we ask any thing according to his will, he heareth us: and if we know that he hear us, whatsoever we ask, we know that we have the petitions that we desired of him

GREEK WORDS

1. "ask" — αἰτέω (*aiteo*): to put forth a well-stated, specific petition to request assistance, and this word foremost has to do with asking for assistance with physical or tangible needs
2. "receive" — λαμβάνω (*lambano*): I receive or I take
3. "because" — διότι (*dioti*): a conjunction that walks the reader into the very clear reason he or she has experienced failure in prayer
4. "amiss" — κακῶς (*kakos*): badly, improperly, or wrongly

SYNOPSIS

In our first lesson, we saw that one of the causes for hindered or delayed answers to prayer is praying inconsistently. When we vacillate, flip-flopping back and forth in what we are praying, it doesn't get us anywhere. In fact, if we are constantly wavering in our prayers, believing God's promises one moment and doubting them the next, the Bible says it's like getting caught in a destructive riptide which drags us out to sea and drowns us. If we are going to receive God's answers, we need to ask and keep on asking Him for what we need in faith.

The emphasis of this lesson:

There's a right way and a wrong way to pray. Praying incorrectly will hinder us from receiving answers to our prayers. Therefore, it is essential that we pray correctly, which means praying scripturally and in agreement with God's Word. When we pray for things God promises in His Word, we can pray confidently and boldly, knowing He will answer.

Praying Incorrectly Hinders Our Prayers

As we've noted, God wants to bless everyone. Jesus said that the Father, "…Maketh his sun to rise on the evil and on the good, and sendeth rain on the just and on the unjust" (Matthew 5:45). Isn't it interesting that God doesn't say He is only going to let the sun shine on the good. Instead, He causes it to shine on both good and evil people and sends rain on the just and on the unjust. Indeed, He is a merciful and generous God.

Nevertheless, when it comes to answering prayer, there are several factors that can cause our prayers to go unanswered or for God's answers to be delayed. In addition to praying inconsistently, *praying incorrectly* can also hold up or block answers to our prayers.

Like Rick, maybe you grew up in a church or denomination that didn't believe in certain things that the Bible teaches. For example, his church really didn't believe in healing, and as a result, they would often pray for people to die peacefully. But that was an incorrect prayer, and when we pray incorrectly, we are not going to receive the answers God promises us in His Word.

We Have a Right To Ask God To Meet Our Tangible Needs

James, the half-brother of Jesus, identified the problem of praying incorrectly in his letter to First Century believers. He said:

Ye ask, and receive not, because ye ask amiss....
— James 4:3

Notice the word "ask" in this verse. It is a form of the Greek word *aiteo*, and it means *to put forth a well-stated, specific petition to request assistance*. This word primarily has to do with *asking for assistance with physical or tangible needs*, which means if you have a physical, tangible need, such as financial provision, fuel for your car, or food and clothing for your family, you have a right to present those specific needs to God.

Equally important, the word *aiteo* — translated here as "ask" — also carries with it *a full expectation that you are going to get a positive response for what you are asking*. The use of this word *aiteo* informs us that if a believer knows and is confident of what the Bible promises, he can confidently, boldly, and frankly pray because he knows that what he is requesting is based on God's Word.

Apparently, James' audience was fiercely fighting in the flesh to resolve difficulties, and they were warring to get what they desired. But in the process, they had forgotten to pray and ask for God's physical and tangible assistance. As often happens, they had taken matters into their own hands instead of taking the matters to God in faith, believing Him to answer them.

If they had gone to God to present their specific prayer petitions and had trusted Him, their matters could have been resolved earlier by answered prayer. But by taking only a fleshly approach to obtain what they needed or wanted, they failed; for the flesh is utterly powerless and completely unable to fully meet its own needs without the assistance of God and His promises.

Once We Ask, We Must Also 'Receive'

Looking again at James 4:3, it says, "Ye ask, and receive not, because ye ask amiss...." What is interesting here is that the word "not" in Greek is *an emphatic no*, which means we will emphatically *not* receive an answer to our prayers "because we ask amiss."

The word "receive" is a form of the Greek word *lambano*, and it means *I receive* or *I take*. It describes what is freely given but must be received or taken by faith. When God gives something, one must use his faith to receive it. God is continuously giving to people, but they do not receive His gifts because they are not using their faith to take what He is attempting to give them.

Everything that comes from God — including our salvation — is a gift that is freely given but it must be received or taken by faith. In a practical sense, a good friend could be holding a $100 bill in his hand and offering it to you as a gift. But in order for you to benefit from the gift he is offering, you have to reach out your own hand and take the $100. In the same way, you need to reach out in faith and receive, or take, the answer to your prayer that God is offering.

Why Do We Often *Not* Receive What We Ask For?

Scripture says that we receive not "because ye ask amiss…" (James 4:3). The word "because" here is the Greek word *dioti*, a conjunction that walks the reader into the very clear reason for why he has experienced failure in prayer, and that reason is because he has been asking "amiss." In Greek, the word "amiss" is *kakos*, which means *badly*, *improperly*, or *wrongly*.

Make no mistake: when a petition is made, it must be based on what the Bible promises and not on what we simply want to see happen in our lives. Hence, before a prayerful petition is made, we must first discover what *is* and *isn't* promised in God's Word so that we don't ask *amiss* — for asking correctly or incorrectly determines what will transpire.

Take physical health, for example. God desires us to have good health and promises it in His Word, so praying for health is correct — not amiss. Likewise, God's Word promises prosperity, so asking Him to prosper us is praying correctly, not amiss. We see this in Third John 2 and Deuteronomy 29:9. When we pray according to God's Word, we are praying correctly. He honors His promises and our faith, and thus, when we make a specific, prayerful petition, it must be done in accordance with the Word of God and submitted to Him in faith.

When we factor in the original Greek meaning of the key words in this portion of James 4:3, the *Renner Interpretive Version* (*RIV*) is as follows:

> **And even when you do put out a prayer petition, you don't receive what you're seeking because of the unmistakable fact that you're making your petition badly, improperly, and wrongly...**

So How Do We Pray Correctly?

One of the most powerful and important passages you need to know and commit to memory regarding how to pray correctly is First John 5:14 and 15, which says:

> **And this is the confidence that we have in him, that, if we ask any thing according to his will, he heareth us: and if we know that he hear us, whatsoever we ask, we know that we have the petitions that we desired of him.**

Notice it says, "if we ask anything according to his will, *he heareth us.*" When you know you are praying according to His will, it gives you boldness and confidence. And this verse says if you pray according to His will — which is His Word — *He hears you!* Thus, praying (asking God for something) in accordance with His Word is not taking a stab in the dark or making an educated guess. On the contrary, it is hitting the bull's eye of His will.

When you align yourself with God's Word, you are agreeing with Him, and as you do, you can present your request from a very confident, bold position. You are not standing on your own intellect, ideas, or insights. You are standing firmly on the promises of the Word of God.

This truth should make you pause regularly and ask yourself, *How much Scripture is in my prayers?* Remember: God listens for His Word when you pray. Hence, your prayers should be saturated in His Word. When you get in line with the Word, the divine answers you need will get to you quicker.

What Is Your Need?

This brings us to the all-important question: *what do you need?* Do you need *healing*? Then you need to dive into the Word of God and find out what God says about healing. There's no need to play the guessing game another day. You can know exactly what God says about healing, and when you learn what He has promised, you can lock in on it and pray those promises. In time, His healing will be yours.

Do you need *restoration in a relationship?* There are many relational conflicts in society today. Many husbands and wives need to be reconciled to each other, and the same is true for many parents and children. God's will regarding relationships is clearly defined in Scripture — unity and peace among people are His heart's desire (*see* Psalm 133). So finding out what He has promised about restoration is vital for your relationships.

Maybe you need a good *job* or *financial provision* to pay your bills. Answers to both issues can be found in God's Word. Clearly, God doesn't want anyone to be poor, which is why Jesus said He came that we might have an abundant life (*see* John 10:10). If you'll do some digging in your Bible's concordance, which is often in the back pages, or use an online Bible search engine, you will find verses that talk about finances and work. As a result, you will be able to pray correctly and receive what you need from the Lord.

Then there is *forgiveness*. So many people today walk around with unforgiveness and bitterness in their heart, and when they pray for those who hurt them, they often ask God to "get them" by pouring out His judgement on them. But prayers like these are incorrect, and God cannot respond to them. People forgiving one another is what His Word advocates. It is filled with promises about forgiveness and what happens when we choose to forgive.

Lock Out the World and Lock In on the Word!

Friend, you don't just have to have a "hope so" kind of faith that merely wishes for good things to happen. You can know what God promises in His Word and lock your faith in on what He says. This will give you boldness and confidence when you pray. What He says in His Word is His will, and when you stand on His Word in prayer, God will move in your life.

Whatever you do, don't fill your mind and heart with the depressing and discouraging messages that bombard a great deal of the TV airwaves, social media, and the internet. The philosophies and opinions of this world will drain you of joy, fill you with unbelief, and diminish the power of God's Word in your life.

It will also cause you to pray amiss, and God is not obligated to answer your incorrect prayers. He is listening for His Word — that is what He responds to. When He hears you pray His Word, He'll release His power into your situations. So, get into the Word of God and find out what He says about each challenge you are facing. Then pray according to Scripture. When you're praying in agreement with the will of God (God's Word), it guarantees that He hears you, and you will receive a "YES!" to your request.

STUDY QUESTIONS

> **Study to shew thyself approved unto God, a workman that needeth not to be ashamed, rightly dividing the word of truth.**
> **— 2 Timothy 2:15**

1. When it comes to meeting your needs, it is imperative to remember that your flesh is utterly powerless and completely unable to fully meet your own needs and win against the enemy without the assistance of God. Look at what the Bible says about your flesh's ability apart from God. What is the Holy Spirit showing you in these passages?
   - Zechariah 4:6
   - Psalm 127:1,2 and Second Chronicles 20:12
   - Romans 7:18 and John 6:63
   - Philippians 3:3
   - John 15:5 and Second Corinthians 3:4,5

2. Praying correctly means praying *in agreement with God's Word*. Whatever God promises in the pages of Scripture, we can confidently petition Him for in prayer. That is what He instructs us to do in Isaiah 62:6 (*AMPC*). Carefully reflect on this verse below and commit it to memory. How does hearing and knowing this truth inspire you to adjust your prayers?
   …You who [are His servants and by your prayers] put the Lord in remembrance [of His promises], keep not silence.

3. The truth of Isaiah 62:6 should make you pause and ask yourself, *How much Scripture is in my prayers?* Once you answer honestly, pray and ask the Holy Spirit, "What can I do to get more of the Word of God in me? What can I eliminate from my daily routine to make more

time to saturate myself in the Word?" Be still and listen. What is He saying to you?

PRACTICAL APPLICATION

> But be ye doers of the word, and not hearers only, deceiving your own selves.
> —James 1:22

1. In the current challenge(s) you are facing, have you taken matters into your own hands instead of taking matters to God in faith, believing He will answer? Are there any adjustments you sense you need to make in what you are doing? If so, what are they?
2. When a prayer petition is made, it must be based on what God promises in His Word and not only on what we want to happen in our lives. Take a few moments to jot down the top three things you are asking God for in prayer. Are these requests in agreement with God's Word? If so, write out the verses that back up your requests. This will strengthen your faith and empower you with confidence to boldly believe God will answer your prayers.
3. Have you ever heard someone pray a bold, audacious prayer and been offended by it? Did you think they were arrogant and presumptuous to pray such a prayer? How is this lesson shedding a new light on those kinds of prayers?

LESSON 3

TOPIC

A Lack of Faith Can Hinder Prayers From Being Answered

SCRIPTURES

1. **Matthew 5:45** — That ye may be the children of your Father which is in heaven: for he maketh his sun to rise on the evil and on the good, and sendeth rain on the just and on the unjust.

2. **Mark 9:23** — Jesus said unto him, If thou canst believe, all things are possible to him that believeth.
3. **Romans 4:20,21** — He staggered not at the promise of God through unbelief; but was strong in faith, giving glory to God; and being fully persuaded that, what he had promised, he was able also to perform.
4. **Romans 12:3** — For I say, through the grace given unto me, to every man that is among you, not to think of himself more highly than he ought to think; but to think soberly, according as God hath dealt to every man the measure of faith.
5. **Romans 10:17** — So then faith cometh by hearing, and hearing by the word of God.
6. **Jude 20** — But ye, beloved, building up yourselves on your most holy faith, praying in the Holy Ghost.
7. **1 Timothy 4:8** — For bodily exercise profiteth little: but godliness is profitable unto all things, having promise of the life that now is, and of that which is to come.
8. **James 2:22** — Seest thou how faith wrought with his works, and by works was faith made perfect?
9. **James 2:26** — For as the body without the spirit is dead, so faith without works is dead also.

GREEK WORDS

No Greek words were shown on the TV program.

SYNOPSIS

All of us experience challenges in life, and those challenges move us to pray. We know from Scripture that "The eyes of the Lord are upon the righteous, and his ears are open unto their cry" (Psalm 34:15). The question is, *Why are answers to our prayers sometimes hindered or delayed?*

So far, we have seen that praying inconsistently and praying incorrectly are two things that detrimentally affect our prayers. A third adverse factor is praying with a lack of faith, which is what we will focus on in this lesson.

The emphasis of this lesson:

Anything is possible to you if you have faith and truly believe God can do it through you. Three primary ways to grow your faith include a

steady practice of hearing God's Word, praying in the Holy Spirit, and exercising your faith.

Anything Is Possible if We Will Believe

As we begin this lesson, let's review what Jesus said about how our heavenly Father operates. He said that when it comes to blessing and taking care of people, "…[God] maketh his sun to rise on the evil and on the good, and sendeth rain on the just and on the unjust" (Matthew 5:45).

This tells us that if God had His way, He would bless everybody because He is a Blesser. However, there are factors that stop us from receiving His blessings, and one of those factors is having a lack of faith. This spiritual condition could be described as a clogged pipeline between us and the Father, where our lack of faith acts prevents His answers from flowing to us.

The good news is that we can make adjustments to our lives that reopen this pipeline so that we can receive God's blessings once again. If we lack faith, there are practical steps we can take to increase our faith and see God do what seems to be impossible.

Think about the instance in the Bible when a father brought his son who was bound by an evil spirit to Jesus. When the man asked the Lord to heal his boy, Jesus told him:

> **…If thou canst believe, all things are possible to him that believeth.**
> **— Mark 9:23**

Indeed, there is nothing that is impossible for God to do in us or through us if we believe. All things are possible — everything is in the realm of probability — to us as we believe and put our faith in Christ. Keep in mind, these are Jesus' words, not man's words.

Now, you might not have thought of this, but if you turn this principle around, the opposite is also true: "If you don't believe, nothing will be possible to you!"

Doing the Impossible Requires Us To First Prepare Ourselves

Rick shared how when God gives him a new directive for his ministry or family that seems impossible, he immediately begins to work on his mind. He knows that he must renew his mind to what God has asked him to do. If God has told Rick to do something — regardless of how big it seems — he needs to adjust his thinking and make sure he is thinking and saying what God thinks and says!

Furthermore, Rick has learned that if he can get his faith level up to where it needs to be, there is literally nothing impossible for him. Strengthening his faith includes making sure he surrounds himself with people who speak faith. And that is what Jesus did when He went to Jairus' house to raise his daughter back to life.

The Bible says that as soon as the Lord arrived at Jairus' house, He "put out" all the professional mourners and the negative naysayers that were in the room. In Greek, the words "put out" are taken from the word *ekballo*, which means *to throw out* or *evict*. Raising the dead girl back to life was a major miracle that would require much faith. Thus, Jesus had no room for doubt, unbelief, and all the boisterous commotion going on in the house. So, he evicted such people from the premises before praying.

Likewise, when you're launching out to do something bigger than you've ever done before, you need to remove all voices of doubt and unbelief and surround yourself with people who operate in faith and with people that have done something impossible themselves. The Renner family is a living example of the fact that there's nothing you can't do if you truly believe God can do it through you.

How Does a Person Get Faith and Strengthen Their Faith?

At this point, you may be thinking, *Well how do I get faith?* That's a great question, and God answers it through the apostle Paul in his letter to the believers in Rome. He said:

> **For I say, through the grace given unto me, to every man that is among you, not to think of himself more highly than he ought**

to think; but to think soberly, according as God hath dealt to every man the measure of faith.

— Romans 12:3

Did you catch that? The Bible says that God has dealt (or given) to every human being a measure of faith. Therefore, everyone — including *you* — has been given faith. In other words, you have the ability to believe and trust God just as much as anyone else on the planet. Even if you feel your faith is the size of a mustard seed, Jesus said it is still enough faith to move mountains (*see* Matthew 17:20).

Now, what happens to your faith once you've received it is up to you. To see it develop and grow strong, you have to do something with it. The apostle Paul tells us that this is how Abraham strengthened his faith. Specifically, Paul said:

He staggered not at the promise of God through unbelief; but was strong in faith, giving glory to God; and being fully persuaded that, what he had promised, he was able also to perform.
— Romans 4:20,21

When it says that Abraham was *strong in faith*, the word "strong" carries the idea of *daily growing strong*. Day by day, his faith was getting stronger and stronger, giving glory to God. It also says that Abraham was *fully persuaded* that what God had promised He was also able to perform. As Abraham waited and trusted God to make him a great nation as He had promised, he grew in his faith. Likewise, as you wait and trust God to do what He said He would do, your faith will grow too.

3 Ways To Grow Your Faith

So now that we know all of us have been given faith and we can see our faith grow, the next logical question would be, *how do we make it grow?* The Bible speaks clearly of three primary ways to grow our faith.

#1: Hear the Word of God

First and foremost, we can increase our faith by *hearing God's Word*. Romans 10:17 tells us:

So then faith cometh by hearing, and hearing by the word of God.

What is very important to note about this verse is that in the original Greek, the word *hearing* is an ongoing action. Thus, it would be better translated, "So then faith cometh by *hearing* and *hearing* and *hearing* and *hearing*…." This tells us that our faith grows bigger and bigger and becomes stronger and stronger the more we hear the Word. The ongoing practice of feeding our spirit and soul with God's Word increases and expands our faith.

Friend, there is no need for you to struggle with your faith. Just begin to make the choice to feed your spirit and soul the Word of God. Turn off the TV and stop endlessly scrolling on social media and develop the healthy habit of hearing and hearing the truth of God's Word. You can read the Bible out loud, listen to the Word on a Bible app, or hear the Word taught by a variety of anointed Bible teachers. The more you hear the Word, the stronger your faith will grow.

#2: Pray in the Holy Spirit

The second way we can increase our faith is by *praying in the Holy Spirit*. God makes this clear in Jude 20 with these instructions:

> **But ye, beloved, building up yourselves on your most holy faith, praying in the Holy Ghost.**

When the Bible says, "praying in the Holy Ghost," it is talking about praying in the spiritual prayer language given by the Holy Spirit, which is also called *praying in tongues*. This is a spiritual gift that comes to us when we are baptized in the Holy Spirit. There are examples of people experiencing this baptism all through the book of Acts, and it began on the Day of Pentecost when 120 followers of Christ were united in prayer in the Upper Room in Jerusalem and the Holy Spirit was poured out on them in the most powerful way ever (*see* Acts 2:1-4).

If you have received the baptism in the Holy Spirit, take time to regularly pray in tongues. Jude 20 says that when you pray in the language of the Holy Spirit, *you build up your faith*. The enemy will try to convince you that praying in tongues is not real, it sounds silly, and it doesn't make a difference. But those are all lies. Praying in tongues *is real*, and *it does make a world of difference* in your life, which is why Satan is trying to get you to give it up.

The next time you begin to feel weak in your faith, get alone and begin to pray in tongues, and your faith will be strengthened. In those moments when you don't know what to pray or how to pray, the Spirit of God Himself will pray through you. The Bible says:

> **And the Holy Spirit helps us in our weakness. For example, we don't know what God wants us to pray for. But the Holy Spirit prays for us with groanings that cannot be expressed in words. And the Father who knows all hearts knows what the Spirit is saying, for the Spirit pleads for us believers in harmony with God's own will.**
> — Romans 8:26,27 (*NLT*)

When you pray in tongues, the Spirit of God is praying a perfect prayer through you — a prayer that is in harmony with God's will for your life. Furthermore, as you pray in the spirit, the Bible says it will bring you into and keep you in the love of God (*see* Jude 21).

#3: Exercise Your Faith

The third way we can increase and grow our faith is by *exercising it*. Our faith is like a muscle, and if we don't use it, we will lose it. Muscles that aren't exercised wither and weaken. But when they are exercised regularly, they grow stronger. We see this principle in First Timothy 4:8, which says:

> **For bodily exercise profiteth little: but godliness is profitable unto all things, having promise of the life that now is, and of that which is to come.**

While physical exercise certainly benefits our body — which is the temple of the Holy Spirit (*see* 1 Corinthians 6:19) — spiritual exercise, described in this verse as *godliness*, is even more profitable because it benefits us now in this present life and in the life to come.

As you exercise your faith, trusting God and believing His Word moment by moment, situation through situation, your faith will be strengthened. If you feel your faith is not ready for something big, start with something small. Believe God's Word instead of believing what you think, how you feel, or what others are saying. Your faith will grow stronger as you flex and use your spiritual muscles.

Faith Must Have Actions

The Bible says that God considered Abraham righteous because of his obedient actions. When God told Abraham to sacrifice his son Isaac, Abraham promptly obeyed by getting up early the next morning and making his way with Isaac to Mount Moriah where he would carry out God's instructions. Scripture says:

> **Seest thou how faith wrought with his works, and by works was faith made perfect?**
> — James 2:22

This verse states that Abraham's faith and his actions worked together, and as a result, his faith was made complete. When we factor in the original Greek meaning of the key words in this verse, the *Renner Interpretive Version* (*RIV*) of James 2:22 is as follows:

> **Don't you see so very clearly that Abraham's rock-solid, unwavering faith worked together with his actions — deeds and works? And don't you also see that it was by his works — that is, his faith that was working in sync with his works — that his faith advanced, matured, and reached its fulfillment?**

In the same way, you must put your faith to work by exercising it and doing what God has instructed. This is confirmed by James four verses later, where he tells us:

> **For as the body without the spirit is dead, so faith without works is dead also.**
> — James 2:26

When we factor in the original Greek meaning of the key words in this verse, the *Renner Interpretive Version* (*RIV*) of James 2:26 is:

> **Also, just exactly as the human body separated from the human spirit is nothing more than a lifeless corpse, in the same exact way also, faith separated from works is absolutely as dead as a corpse.**

Faith must have actions. There is no such thing as passive faith — only active faith. Interestingly, the Greek word for "faith" in the New Testament describes something that has been propelled forward, like a bullet shot out of a gun. Hence, faith is always moving forward and is never in retreat.

If all you're doing is going through life saying, "I believe what God says," but you never back up your belief with actions, there is no proof of your faith. Your actions prove what you really believe. Faith works in sync with actions, and as you begin to put your faith to work, you'll grow, strengthen, mature, and expand your faith.

A Quick Recap of What We Learned

So according to Romans 12:3, everyone has faith — including you. And according to Romans 4:20 and 21, even if your faith seems small, you can grow it, just like Abraham did. The three ways to grow, expand, and increase your faith are:

- **Continually hearing and receiving the Word of God (*see* Romans 10:17).**
- **Regularly praying in the Holy Spirit (*see* Jude 20).**
- **Exercising your faith (*see* 1 Timothy 4:8), which means putting your faith to work (*see* James 2:22, 26).**

Faith is never passive but active. Faith expresses and demonstrates itself through actions, demanding an answer from God. Remember, Jesus said, "…If thou canst believe, all things are possible to him that believeth" (Mark 9:23). If you have prayed and are not receiving an answer to your prayers, begin to take action by carrying out the steps covered in this lesson, and your faith will come alive!

STUDY QUESTIONS

> **Study to shew thyself approved unto God, a workman that needeth not to be ashamed, rightly dividing the word of truth.**
> **— 2 Timothy 2:15**

1. When God asks us to do what seems impossible, we must first prepare ourselves, and that preparation begins with renewing our mind with the truth of God's Word (*see* Romans 12:2). Take some time to look up these verses and learn what you can expect the Word of God to do in your life as you regularly take it in.
    - Hebrews 4:12; John 8:31,32; and James 1:21-25
    - Psalm 119:9; John 17:17; and Ephesians 5:26

- Second Timothy 3:16,17 and Acts 20:32
2. The ongoing practice of feeding your spirit and soul with God's Word increases and expands your faith. What are you presently doing each day to feed yourself God's Word? Is it working? Are you growing in your knowledge and understanding of how God thinks and acts?
3. If what you are doing is not working, pause and pray: "Holy Spirit, what can I do differently to help me gain and retain more of the truth of God's Word?" Be still and listen. What is the Lord showing you?

PRACTICAL APPLICATION

> But be ye doers of the word, and not hearers only, deceiving your own selves.
> — James 1:22

1. Another way for you to grow your faith is to regularly pray in the Holy Spirit, which is a prayer language you receive when you are baptized in the Holy Spirit. Have you experienced the gift of the Spirit's baptism? If you have, are you praying in tongues regularly? If not, why?
2. If you have not received the baptism in the Holy Spirit, you can! Jesus said this gift is yours for the asking and tells you how to receive the Spirit's baptism in Luke 11:9-13. Take some time to read this passage and ask Jesus to baptize you in His Holy Spirit. You can also call RENNER Ministries at 1-800-742-5593 and one of our team members will be happy to pray with you to receive this magnificent gift!

LESSON 4

TOPIC
A Negative Confession Can Hinder Prayers From Being Answered

SCRIPTURES
1. **Matthew 5:45** — That ye may be the children of your Father which is in heaven: for he maketh his sun to rise on the evil and on the good, and sendeth rain on the just and on the unjust.
2. **Mark 11:23,24** — For verily I say unto you, That whosoever shall say unto this mountain, Be thou removed, and be thou cast into the sea; and shall not doubt in his heart, but shall believe that those things which he saith shall come to pass; he shall have whatsoever he saith. Therefore I say unto you, What things soever ye desire, when ye pray, believe that ye receive them, and ye shall have them.
3. **Matthew 12:37** — For by thy words thou shalt be justified, and by thy words thou shalt be condemned.
4. **Proverbs 13:2,3** — A man shall eat good by the fruit of his mouth: but the soul of the transgressors shall eat violence. He that keepeth his mouth keepeth his life: but he that openeth wide his lips shall have destruction.
5. **Proverbs 18:21** — Death and life are in the power of the tongue: and they that love it shall eat the fruit thereof.
6. **Matthew 12:34** — O generation of vipers, how can ye, being evil, speak good things? for out of the abundance of the heart the mouth speaketh.

GREEK WORDS
No Greek words were shown on the TV program.

SYNOPSIS
Thus far, we have seen several factors that can work against us and prevent us from receiving answers to our prayers. In Lesson 1, we identified

praying inconsistently, and in Lesson 2 we talked about praying incorrectly. Both are problems that can hinder or delay our prayers from being answered. A lack of faith can also negatively impact our prayers, which is what we examined in Lesson 3. In this lesson, we will examine a fourth major factor that often prevents us from receiving what we need from God, and that is *a negative confession*.

The emphasis of this lesson:

To engage your faith, you must engage your mouth and eliminate negative confessions. Rock-solid answers to your prayers will come to you as you get your heart and mouth into agreement with God's Word. Believing His Word in your heart and then speaking it with your mouth releases His authority and power in your situation.

What Does a Negative Confession Look Like?

Looking again at our anchor verse, Jesus said, "…[God] maketh his sun to rise on the evil and on the good, and sendeth rain on the just and on the unjust" (Matthew 5:45). That is how our Heavenly Father operates. If He had His way and nothing — including our words and actions — would hinder Him, He would bless and help everyone.

However, there are things in our lives that can hinder us from receiving what God has for us, and one of the blockades to receiving His blessings is a negative confession. If you pray a faith-filled prayer from the Word of God but then, when you're finished praying, you begin to talk negatively, you will actually nullify or cancel what you just prayed.

For example, let's say you need healing in your body, and you pray, "Lord, I know Your Word says in Isaiah 53:5 and First Peter 2:24 that by the stripes Jesus received on His body I am healed. So, I pray right now that my health would be fully restored through Christ. In Jesus' name. Amen." This is praying correctly and in faith — a prayer that God is ready to answer.

But if after you finish praying, you run into a friend and say, "Man, I'm just not feeling any better. I have prayed, but I just don't know that I am healed." With your own words, you just canceled your prayer and confession to God.

To experience rock-solid answers to your prayers, you have to get your heart and your mouth into agreement — you must believe God's Word in your heart and then speak it with your mouth. When the heart and mouth get into agreement, it creates a conduit through which God's power and answers come to us.

Speaking Releases Authority

One of the greatest Bible teachers in recent times was a man by the name of Kenneth Hagin Sr., and the passage of Scripture he is probably most known for expounding on is Mark 11:23,24. In this passage, Jesus powerfully declared:

> **For verily I say unto you, That whosoever shall say unto this mountain, Be thou removed, and be thou cast into the sea; and shall not doubt in his heart, but shall believe that those things which he saith shall come to pass; he shall have whatsoever he saith. Therefore I say unto you, What things soever ye desire, when ye pray, believe that ye receive them, and ye shall have them.**

First, notice the word "verily" in verse 23. When Jesus says, "For verily I say unto you," it is the equivalent of Him saying, "For sure! Listen to this! It is a guarantee!"

The second important aspect about this passage is that Jesus uses the word "say" or "saith" three times. This clearly demonstrates that to engage your faith you must engage your mouth. Notice, He didn't say, "Whosoever shall *think* unto this mountain...." Rather, He said, "Whosoever shall SAY unto this mountain, be thou removed and be thou cast into the sea."

When you encounter opposition from the enemy, you can't just sit silently and *think* your way to victory. You have to open your mouth and *speak* to the opposition. Why? Because **your voice is your authority**. Until you have spoken, you have not released any authority. But when you speak, your authority is released.

Jesus also said, "Whosoever shall say unto this *mountain*...." The "mountain" He is talking about is anything that's creating a problem in your life — anything not of God that you'd like to get rid of.

Words Are Very Important

God was the first to demonstrate the power of words. In the beginning, at the time of creation, God opened His mouth and spoke into existence everything that we see. From the unseen, He created the seen, and He did it with words!

For us, salvation comes with our words. When we confess with our mouth that Jesus is Lord, we are saved. Romans 10:10 says, "For with the heart man believeth unto righteousness; and *with the mouth* confession is made unto salvation."

So, the words of our mouth are very important. The choice to use our voice and speak words that are in agreement with God is what releases His divine authority in our lives. We will examine this principle more closely in just a few moments. But first, let's answer an important question that many people ask regarding Mark 11:23,24.

What Does It Mean to 'Doubt in Your Heart'?

Again, Jesus declared, "…That whosoever shall say unto this mountain, Be thou removed, and be thou cast into the sea; and shall not doubt in his heart, but shall believe that those things which he saith shall come to pass; he shall have whatsoever he saith" (Mark 11:23).

To understand what it means to *doubt in your heart*, we look to the original Greek meaning of the word "doubt," which in this passage would better be translated as *differ*. There are people who say the right thing with their mouth, but in their heart, they are saying and believing something *different*. They may correctly speak and pray what God's Word says, but in their heart, they are imagining and believing the opposite.

That is what Jesus was telling us not to do. Rather than say the right thing with our mouth and then believe something different in our heart, He is telling us that **our mouth and our heart need to be in agreement**. If we're just saying what's right with our mouth, but our heart doesn't believe it, all we're doing is speaking empty words. If that is the case, it is the reason our right confession isn't producing the right results.

Now the truth is, it is much easier to say what is right than to believe what is right. Thus, it may take some time for your mouth and your heart to get into agreement. This is especially true if you've been taught the wrong thing, and in the depth of your heart, you've been believing the wrong thing for a long, long time.

Jesus said when your mouth and your heart line up and you speak to the mountain (or problem), it is going to move.

Your Words During and After Prayer Are Equally Important

What Jesus said in Mark 11:23 and 24 about the connection between our mouth and our faith is reminiscent of what He taught about our words in Matthew 12:37:

> **For by thy words thou shalt be justified, and by thy words thou shalt be condemned.**

This is a very sobering statement from Jesus. The words we speak will either justify us (prove us to be right) or condemn us (prove us to be guilty). This stark warning punctuates our need to very carefully choose our words.

If you want to experience a blessed life that is filled with good things, then you need to get your mouth in agreement with your prayers. If you pray for blessings, don't start speaking curses upon yourself. You can't say or pray for one thing and then walk away and speak words of doubt over what you just said. Saying the right things after you leave prayer is just as important as what you say while you are praying!

Disciplining the Mouth Takes Time

Out of all the books of the Bible, Proverbs probably has the most instruction concerning our words. Take these two related verses for example:

> **The heart of the righteous studieth to answer....**
> — **Proverbs 15:28**

And...

> **The heart of the wise teacheth his mouth, and addeth learning to his lips.**
> — **Proverbs 16:23**

In both passages, we see that a person who is righteous and one who is wise both have truth in their hearts, but their mouths need to be disciplined. It is the heart of the righteous and the heart of the wise that *studies the right way to answer* and *teaches their mouth the right things to stay.* Studying and teaching indicate a process of training the mouth that takes time.

The bottom line is that you can't just speak whatever thoughts and feelings fall into your head. By the power of the Holy Spirit who lives in you, you need to study and teach your mouth how to speak the truth and be in agreement with your heart.

What You Speak You Will Also 'Eat'

You may have heard it said that you are what you eat. Well, according to Scripture, you will also eat what you speak. This principle is found in at least two places in Proverbs. Proverbs 13:2 says:

A man shall eat good by the fruit of his mouth….

This verse says that the words you speak determine what you're going to experience in your life. It doesn't matter how positive you are praying, if you walk around speaking all kinds of negative things about your circumstances, yourself, and your future, you are going to "eat" (experience) what you're saying.

To make sure we understand this vital principle, God expands this meaning in the very next verse:

He that keepeth his mouth keepeth his life: but he that openeth wide his lips shall have destruction.
— **Proverbs 13:3**

The first part of this passage reveals the greatest reward of learning to control our mouth — we preserve and save our very life. The second part of the verse reveals the greatest tragedy of living with a mouth that is out of control — we reap destruction. Can you think of a person who has no filter and says any ole thing that comes to mind? How would you describe their life?

As you consider what their life is like, also consider what the Bible says in Proverbs 18:21:

Death and life are in the power of the tongue: and they that love it shall eat the fruit thereof.

Are you seeing the similarities among all these verses in Proverbs? Hopefully it is beginning to sink in just how much power is in your words. What you say is either going to feed you — and others — life or death.

Choose What You Believe and What You Say

It may be that God has spoken to your heart and has shown you what He wants to do through you. He may have even revealed some specific scriptures in His Word, and you are standing on them in prayer. Day by day, you have been praying His promises in faith and declaring His assignment over your life.

Don't be surprised if out of nowhere, unexpected challenges begin to manifest. If that happens, continue to pray God's Word and guard your words carefully. The last thing you want to do is walk away from prayer and begin to make statements like, "I sure hope things work out alright. I'm just not so sure they will." Or to say, "It never fails! Something always happens to sabotage God's plans."

These are wrong, negative confessions that will nullify the promises of God you just prayed. Instead of giving a voice to doubt and fear, stay the course and continue to say what you know God has said in His Word and to your heart, regardless of how you feel or what you see. Maintaining a positive confession doesn't mean you're blind to the reality around you. It just means you're choosing what you're going to believe and what you're going to say.

Get Your Heart and Mouth in Agreement with God

Keep in mind that what comes out of your mouth is directly linked to what is in your heart. That is what Jesus said in Matthew 12:34: "…For out of the abundance of the heart the mouth speaketh."

If your heart is filled with God's Word, then it's going to be easier for your mouth and your heart to be in agreement. Unfortunately, many people reverse the order and try to speak the Word first before it is in their hearts, which is why their prayers produce no results.

The key to getting your mouth right is to first get your heart right. This will happen naturally as you continue to feed on God's Word and allow it to fill your heart. Then when you open your mouth to speak, you will speak the truth and be in agreement with your heart. When the heart and mouth are in agreement with God, mountain-moving faith is released!

Once more, take a few moments to really chew on these words from Jesus:

> **For verily I say unto you, That whosoever shall say unto this mountain, Be thou removed, and be thou cast into the sea; and shall not doubt in his heart, but shall believe that those things which he saith shall come to pass; he shall have whatsoever he saith. Therefore I say unto you, What things soever ye desire, when ye pray, believe that ye receive them, and ye shall have them.**
> — Mark 11:23,24

Friend, isn't it high time you learn to monitor your mouth? Take time to pray and invite the Holy Spirit to help you. As you do, He will empower you to get a grip on your lips and bring your heart and mouth into agreement with what God says.

STUDY QUESTIONS

> Study to shew thyself approved unto God, a workman that needeth not to be ashamed, rightly dividing the word of truth.
> — 2 Timothy 2:15

1. Your words are important and powerful. Just as God created the world we see with His words, to a great degree, we create our world with our words. The Bible has much to say about the words of our mouth. Take some time to examine these scriptures and write down what the Holy Spirit shows you about the words you speak.

   - **What is the difference between the mouth of the *wise* and the mouth of a *fool*?**
     See Psalm 37:30; Proverbs 10:11,14,21,32; 14:3; 15:2; 17:27; 18:6,7; and Ecclesiastes 10:12.

   - **What happens when you let your mouth say whatever it wants to say?**
     See Proverbs 10:19 and James 1:26; 3:5-8.

- **What are the blessings of guarding your lips? And what should your speech be like?**
  See Proverbs 13:3; 17:28; 21:23; James 3:2; and Colossians 4:6.
2. If you want to experience a blessed life that is filled with good things, then you need to be very careful about the words you choose. According to Psalm 34:11-14 and First Peter 3:10,11, what does controlling your mouth demonstrate? What promise does God make to us here if we will discipline what we say?
3. God is listening for His Word when we speak — that is what He and His angels respond to. What do Jeremiah 1:12 and Psalm 103:20 say about how God and His angels respond to hearing the Word spoken aloud in our conversations and our prayers?

PRACTICAL APPLICATION

> But be ye doers of the word, and not hearers only,
> deceiving your own selves.
> —James 1:22

1. When you encounter opposition from the enemy, you can't just sit silently and *think* your way to victory. You must open your mouth and *speak* to the opposition. How would you describe your normal response when you are confronted by frustrating challenges? Do you explode in anger? Wish it would just go away? Pray silently? Or do you pray to God and speak His Word over your life and against the enemy? If you are not doing the latter, how do you think things might change if you did?
2. What mountain of problems are you facing right now that you need to speak to? Take time to search the Scriptures for specific promises that refute the lies of the enemy and begin to pray those promises out loud to the Lord, over your life, and against the enemy.

LESSON 5

TOPIC
Bad Relationships Can Hinder Prayers From Being Answered

SCRIPTURES
1. **Matthew 5:45** — That ye may be the children of your Father which is in heaven: for he maketh his sun to rise on the evil and on the good, and sendeth rain on the just and on the unjust.
2. **Mark 11:23-25** — For verily I say unto you, That whosoever shall say unto this mountain, Be thou removed, and be thou cast into the sea; and shall not doubt in his heart, but shall believe that those things which he saith shall come to pass; he shall have whatsoever he saith. Therefore I say unto you, What things soever ye desire, when ye pray, believe that ye receive them, and ye shall have them. And when ye stand praying, forgive, if ye have ought against any: that your Father also which is in heaven may forgive you your trespasses.
3. **Matthew 5:23,24** — Therefore if thou bring thy gift to the altar, and there rememberest that thy brother hath ought against thee; Leave there thy gift before the altar, and go thy way; first be reconciled to thy brother, and then come and offer thy gift.
4. **Hebrews 12:14** — Follow peace with all men, and holiness, without which no man shall see the Lord.

GREEK WORDS
No Greek words were shown on the TV program.

SYNOPSIS
Jesus said that our heavenly Father, "...Maketh his sun to rise on the evil and on the good, and sendeth rain on the just and on the unjust" (Matthew 5:45), which means He desires to bless everyone. But there are certain factors that can delay or even stop us from receiving His blessings. These include praying inconsistently, praying incorrectly, a lack of faith,

and a negative confession. A fifth dynamic that can delay or hinder God from answering our prayers is *bad relationships*.

The emphasis of this lesson:

Life is about relationships. Healthy ones are life-giving, but when we get hurt by others and we hold on to that hurt, unforgiveness sets in and clogs the spiritual pipeline between us and God. To unclog the pipe, we must receive God's grace and fix those relationships.

Get Your Heart and Mouth in Agreement

In Lesson 4, we unpacked the meaning of Jesus' words in Mark 11:23,24. In this passage, the Lord says, "For verily I say unto you, That whosoever shall say unto this mountain, Be thou removed, and be thou cast into the sea; and shall not doubt in his heart, but shall believe that those things which he saith shall come to pass; he shall have whatsoever he saith. Therefore I say unto you, What things soever ye desire, when ye pray, believe that ye receive them, and ye shall have them."

We saw that the Greek word for "doubt" here means *to differ*. So, when Jesus says we are not to doubt in our heart, He is saying we are not to *differ* in our heart. In other words, if we want to have powerful, effective prayers, we are not to say one thing with our mouth but believe something different in our heart. We need to work with the Holy Spirit to bring our mouth and heart into agreement.

Now, if you've been taught the wrong thing, and in the depth of your heart, you've been believing the wrong thing for a long time, it will probably take some time for your mouth and your heart to get into agreement. But it is doable if you ask God for His grace. When your mouth and your heart line up, you will be able to speak to the mountain (or problem) you are facing, and it will move.

Listen and Pay Attention to What the Holy Spirit May Be Showing You

In the very next verse, Jesus goes on to say, "And when ye stand praying, forgive, if ye have ought against any: that your Father also which is in heaven may forgive you your trespasses" (Mark 11:25).

What Jesus is inferring here is that if you have any issues of unforgiveness with anyone, it can hinder your fellowship with the Father. That is, it can clog the spiritual pipeline between you and God, and the answers to prayer that you need cannot get to you.

It's not that God doesn't want to bless you. The problem is that the "debris" of offense that hasn't been dealt with has turned into unforgiveness, and it is cluttering the conduit of your communication with the Father. Hence, when we pray, we need to take time to listen and pay attention to what the Holy Spirit may be showing us.

Deal With the Offenses You Have With Anyone

How are we supposed to deal with an offense with a brother or sister in Christ? Jesus tells us clearly in Matthew 5:23,24:

> **Therefore if thou bring thy gift to the altar, and there rememberest that thy brother hath ought against thee;**
>
> **Leave there thy gift before the altar, and go thy way; first be reconciled to thy brother, and then come and offer thy gift.**

In this passage, Jesus is talking about a believer who is praying and asking God for His help in exchange for something. The *gift* he or she brings to the altar could be worship, a financial gift, or a vow to do something specific for the Lord.

If you are worshiping God, praying and asking Him to do something for you in exchange for a gift, and you suddenly remember that another believer is holding an offense toward you — or that you are holding an offense toward someone — that may be the Holy Spirit alerting you that something is blocking your prayers.

Jesus said, "Leave there thy gift before the altar, and go thy way; first be reconciled to thy brother, and then come and offer thy gift" (Matthew 5:24). If the Spirit of God is telling you to get a relationship right, then do it as quickly as you can! Ignoring what He is saying may affect your ability to receive what you need from Heaven. Indeed, if you want your prayers to be answered, it is crucial for you to keep your relationships right.

Denise's Personal Example of Identifying and Working Through Unforgiveness

If you are living and breathing, you are going to experience offense. Jesus said it is impossible to avoid (*see* Luke 17:1). We are all imperfect, and therefore, we will sometimes hurt one another with what we say or do. Denise shared how her book *The Gift of Forgiveness* was born out of a situation in which she was hurt and holding onto unforgiveness. She said:

> There was a time in my life when I had unforgiveness and bitterness lingering in my heart, and I was totally unaware of it. It was bringing sickness into my soul and body, but I did not see the connection to the offense I was harboring inside. My hands and feet were painfully cold all the time, and my mind and emotions were ravaged by overwhelming fear and even panic attacks.
>
> Day after day, I was seeking the Lord, fervently praying, 'God, please deliver me from fear! Heal my hands and feet.' I was desperately trying to rid myself of the physical and mental trauma I was experiencing, but I didn't know how to get rid of it.
>
> Deep inside, I knew that my heart was not right, so I was honest with God about it. It's important that we not be religious with Him and put on a mask in our prayer time. If you have unforgiveness and bitterness in your heart, don't try and cover it with religious words or blame it on another person. That will not make you free — only telling the truth will.
>
> So, there I was — in a place of suffering, pain, and torment from physical problems and panic attacks in which fear would just overtake my mind. Eventually, the Holy Spirit helped me see that I had opened the door to sickness and fear through unforgiveness in my heart. Until that moment, I truly thought, *I am just an angel in this situation. I'm not the one with the problem. They are the one that needs to change.* But the Holy Spirit made it clear that I was the one in the wrong.
>
> When you seek Him, He will talk to you and reveal the truth of what's going on in the situation. That's what He did for me. He revealed the unforgiveness that was in my heart and helped me

forgive the person who hurt me. Although you and I can't change others, God can change us if we're honest and cooperate with Him.

I went to bed that night still battling fear and feeling pain in my hands and feet. But when I woke up the next morning, I was completely free of all adverse symptoms! My hands and my feet were normal, and most of all, my heart and my mind were at peace.

The Bible has much to say about unforgiveness. One of the most important examples of how we are to respond to the mistreatment of others is found in Acts 7 where Stephen was being stoned for simply preaching the Gospel. The Jews became so enraged by what he was sharing that they took him outside of the city and began throwing massive stones at him.

Now you might think that Stephen was thinking, *Oh God, please help me*. But that's not what was on his mind. Just seconds before he died, he cried out, 'Lord Jesus, receive my spirit,' and in the next verse, '...He kneeled down, and cried with a loud voice, Lord, lay not this sin to their charge. And when he had said this, he fell asleep' (Acts 7:60). Amazingly, Stephen released every single person that was there, asking God not to charge them with this crime.

This is the attitude of forgiveness I'm talking about. It's the same attitude Jesus displayed on the Cross just before He died. As blood poured from His body and He gasped for every breath as He painfully pushed His body up on the nail in His feet, He said, '...Father, forgive them; for they know not what they do...' (Luke 23:34).

It's clear from these examples and the teachings of God's Word that there are two positions we as believers can take when it comes to forgiveness: (1) We can pray, 'Father, don't charge this person (or people) with this,' or (2) we can pray, 'Forgive them, Father, because they don't know what they're doing.'

When you release your offender, you open the pipeline of communication between you and God, allowing all that He is, which is all that you need, to flow to you, including His love, freedom, and forgiveness. Don't be like so many Christians who walk around dead because they are harboring unforgiveness and bitterness in their hearts. Choose to forgive and release those who hurt you into God's hands.

Go After Peace and Holiness With All You've Got!

When you go to a person to be reconciled, he or she may not realize they did anything wrong. Likewise, they may not want to be reconciled to you. Either way, how they respond is not your responsibility. Regardless of what they do, you are free. You did what Jesus said to do in Matthew 5:24 and have cleared the clutter out of your own life. The pipeline between you and the Father is now open so you can receive from Heaven.

This brings us to a related verse of Scripture in Hebrews 12:14, which says:

> **Follow peace with all men, and holiness, without which no man shall see the Lord.**

The word "follow" here is very important. It is a form of the Greek word *dioko*, which is a hunting term that means *to run swiftly after something* or *to pursue and track down in a hostile manner*. The tense of this verb is ongoing and would better be translated as *to follow, follow, follow, and follow*. The use of this word indicates that sometimes it is really hard to have peace with people. Nevertheless, it is our job to keep following after peace with all men, regardless of who they are, and do everything we can to capture it.

In addition to following peace, we are also to pursue *holiness* with the same passion. This word "holiness," a form of the Greek word *hagiasmos*, refers to a higher standard of behavior that is far above the rest of the world. That is what God holds us to. Without holiness, no man shall *see* the Lord. That word "see" is also significant because it carries the idea of *being admitted into the immediate presence of someone*. The use of this word means that the latter part of Hebrews 12:14 could be interpreted to say, "Without holiness, no man will experience the Lord or be admitted to His presence."

When you have something in your heart against someone else, it affects your ability to receive answers from Heaven as well as your ability to experience the presence of the Lord. Maybe you have been in a church meeting where you looked around and saw that just about everyone was greatly blessed by God's manifest presence. You, on the other hand, felt absolutely nothing, and as a result you wondered what was wrong with you. Well, it may be that there was an issue of unforgiveness in your heart that needed to be resolved.

So, not only can a bad relationship stop you from receiving the answers you need, but it can also stop you from enjoying God's presence. And friend, you need the presence of the Lord because in His presence there is fullness of joy (*see* Psalm 16:11), and the joy of the Lord is your strength (Nehemiah 8:10).

A Sincere Apology Is Sometimes the Best Response

Keep in mind that as you seek to make things right, you may not know how to fix what's broken in your relationship with that other person. If you find yourself in this situation, you may only be able to say, "I am truly sorry for hurting you in any way," or "I forgive you."

In some cases, the best thing you can say is, "I don't know what happened between us, but I'm sincerely sorry for whatever took place." Whatever the situation may be, pray and ask the Holy Spirit for the right words and the right time to speak, and then simply do the best that you can with His grace.

To be clear, God is not asking you to go on a digging expedition to try and figure out all the wrong things you (or others) ever did in your relationships. What Jesus is saying in Matthew 5:23 and 24 is that if you are worshiping and praying and the Holy Spirit suddenly brings to mind a person that has hurt you or that you have hurt, listen and pay attention to what He is saying. He is telling you there's something in you that's going to affect your ability to receive answers to your prayers.

Ultimately, when you go to that other person, you are not going to deal with *them* — you are going to deal with *you*. You're trying to unclog the debris of offense and unforgiveness from your life and open the spiritual pipeline between you and God. So, if they don't respond the way you think they should, that's okay. It's not about them — *it's about you*. You're trying to get yourself free, so you can receive what you need from the Lord and experience His presence and all His goodness that He wants to bring into your life.

STUDY QUESTIONS

> Study to shew thyself approved unto God, a workman that needeth not to be ashamed, rightly dividing the word of truth.
> — 2 Timothy 2:15

1. Take a few moments to reread Jesus' instructions in Mark 11:25 as well as what He said in Luke 17:3,4 and Matthew 6:14,15. Also read what God wrote through Paul in Ephesians 4:32 and Colossians 3:13. What is the Holy Spirit showing you in all these verses about the vital importance of forgiveness?
2. According to Jesus' words in Matthew 5:23,24, He wants us to do our best to deal with the hurts that we receive from and inflict on others. What additional instruction does Jesus give in Matthew 18:15-17 about dealing with the offenses caused by fellow believers?

PRACTICAL APPLICATION

> But be ye doers of the word, and not hearers only, deceiving your own selves.
> — James 1:22

1. After reading and hearing Denise's story of being sick and filled with fear as a result of holding on to unforgiveness, are there any similarities between what she went through and what you've experienced? If so, what are they? And what is the Holy Spirit revealing to you about your own life?
2. In Acts 24:16 (*AMPC*), Paul said, "Therefore I always exercise and discipline myself [mortifying my body, deadening my carnal affections, bodily appetites, and worldly desires, endeavoring in all respects] to have a clear (unshaken, blameless) conscience, void of offense toward God and toward men." In your own words, what do you think it looks like to "exercise and discipline" yourself in this way? As you answer, also consider what Paul wrote in Ephesians 4:26,27.
3. Have you been praying and then suddenly thought about someone who has a grudge against you, or someone with whom you're holding a grudge? Has reading through this lesson brought a person's face or name to mind? It could be that the Holy Spirit is alerting you of an offense that is clogging the conduit of your communication with God. The person on your mind is a relationship that needs healing. Take

time now to pray and tell the Lord how you feel inside. Ask Him to heal your heart and soul and to give you His grace to go to the person(s) you need to go to and attempt to make peace.

LESSON 6

TOPIC
Spiritual Opposition Can Hinder Prayers From Being Answered

SCRIPTURES
1. **Matthew 5:45** — That ye may be the children of your Father which is in heaven: for he maketh his sun to rise on the evil and on the good, and sendeth rain on the just and on the unjust.
2. **Ephesians 6:12** — For we wrestle not against flesh and blood, but against principalities, against powers, against the rulers of the darkness of this world, against spiritual wickedness in high places.
3. **Daniel 10:2** — In those days I Daniel was mourning three full weeks.
4. **Daniel 10:10-14** — And, behold, an hand touched me, which set me upon my knees and upon the palms of my hands. And he said unto me, O Daniel, a man greatly beloved, understand the words that I speak unto thee, and stand upright: for unto thee am I now sent. And when he had spoken this word unto me, I stood trembling. Then said he unto me, Fear not, Daniel: for from the first day that thou didst set thine heart to understand, and to chasten thyself before thy God, thy words were heard, and I am come for thy words. But the prince of the kingdom of Persia withstood me one and twenty days: but, lo, Michael, one of the chief princes, came to help me; and I remained there with the kings of Persia. Now I am come to make thee understand what shall befall thy people in the latter days: for yet the vision is for many days.
5. **Mark 4:36-39** — And when they had sent away the multitude, they took him even as he was in the ship. And there were also with him other little ships. And there arose a great storm of wind, and the waves beat into the ship, so that it was now full. And he was in the

hinder part of the ship, asleep on a pillow: and they awake him, and say unto him, Master, carest thou not that we perish? And he arose, and rebuked the wind, and said unto the sea, Peace, be still. And the wind ceased, and there was a great calm.

GREEK WORDS
No Greek words were shown on the TV program.

SYNOPSIS
Sometimes the hindrance to our prayers has nothing to do with us. Rather, it has everything to do with our unseen adversary. Second Corinthians 10:3 says, "For though we walk in the flesh, we do not war after the flesh." What we are up against is *spiritual opposition* — a very real, formidable force we must be aware of and contend with.

If you are praying the Word in faith and doing everything you know to do and you are still not seeing answers to your prayers, it may be because the enemy is busy at work behind the scenes. But thankfully, through Christ you have been given authority and power over all the power of the enemy, and nothing shall in any way harm you (*see* Luke 10:19)!

The emphasis of this lesson:

From Genesis to Revelation, the Bible reveals the reality of spiritual opposition. Satan, a fallen angel, along with demonic forces and other angels who rebelled against God, often fights against us to distract, discourage, and derail us from our God-given destiny. But with the strength of God's Spirit living in us, we can take authority over the enemy and receive what we need from Him.

A Quick Review

Thus far, we have identified five things that cause answers to our prayers to be delayed or hindered, and the first one is *praying inconsistently*, which is wavering or vacillating in our prayers. The second factor we saw is *praying incorrectly*, which means not praying in agreement with God's Word.

The third reason for unanswered prayers or delays in receiving what we need is *a lack of faith*. To overcome this, we must grow our faith by hearing God's Word, praying in the Holy Spirit, and exercising our faith. The fourth obstacle that can nullify the effectiveness of our prayers is *a negative confession*. If we will get our heart and mouth into agreement with God's Word, rock-solid answers to our prayers will come.

In our last lesson, we learned about *bad relationships* and how holding on to unforgiveness can really jam the spiritual pipeline between us and God. To overcome this condition, Jesus told us that if, when we are praying, we suddenly think of someone that is holding a grudge against us — or someone with whom we are holding a grudge — we need to go to them and do our best to make things right, and then come back and begin to pray again.

Friend, God wants to answer our prayers. Jesus confirms this in Matthew 5:45, where He said that the Father in Heaven "…maketh his sun to rise on the evil and on the good, and sendeth rain on the just and on the unjust." So, being the good heavenly Father that He is, blessing us and answering our prayers is an inseparable part of His nature. However, there are factors, such as the five we just mentioned, that can delay or even prevent us from receiving answers to our prayers.

What We're Fighting Against Is Spiritual, Not Physical

Spiritual opposition is another major hindrance to our prayers. According to Ephesians 6:12, there will be times in our lives when these ungodly powers fight against us to keep us from victory. That is why the apostle Paul wrote an entire section on spiritual armor — we need spiritual weapons to defeat the enemy! Ephesians 6:12 says the following:

> **For we wrestle not against flesh and blood, but against principalities, against powers, against the rulers of the darkness of this world, against spiritual wickedness in high places.**

Notice Paul said that our struggle is **not** against *flesh and blood*. In other words, it is not against people or things in the natural, physical world. This is very important to realize because we all tend to struggle with what and who we can see and touch. For example, if we have a financial problem, we wrestle with our finances. If we have challenges in our health, we struggle with our body. And if we have a relational problem, we wrestle with people — be it our spouse, children, coworkers, friends, etc.

Although we certainly need to do all that we can do in the natural to resolve our issues, this verse informs us that sometimes what we are up against is unseen spiritual forces working behind the scenes, and because they are not natural, they cannot be defeated by natural means. Again, the verse says, "For we wrestle not against flesh and blood, but against principalities, against powers, against the rulers of the darkness of this world, against spiritual wickedness in high places" (Ephesians 6:12).

Rick's Earliest Encounter With the Unseen Realm

Rick said that the first time he came to understand the reality of the spiritual war we are in was when he was a freshman in college. He had been reading the Word, praying, and growing in his relationship with the Lord, and then suddenly, he hit a period where it felt like there was some kind of blockage he couldn't define or defeat.

Frustrated and confused, he began to cry out to God and ask, "Lord, what is this blockage?" And the Holy Spirit opened his eyes to the realm of the spirit and enabled him to look up and see what looked like a hazy cloud standing between him and the answers to prayer that he needed.

For the first time, he understood that what he saw and what he was up against were spiritual forces. And the Holy Spirit began teaching him how to deal with that unseen opposition. Specifically, the Spirit said, "Begin to rebuke the enemy by opening your mouth and verbally standing against him with the Word."

Rick did just what the Holy Spirit told him to do, and each time he opened his mouth to rebuke the enemy, it was like a burst of light began to break through that hazy cloud standing between him and the answers to prayer he needed. This was a hands-on experience in spiritual warfare that he would learn and draw from for years to come.

The Prophet Daniel Experienced Spiritual Opposition

One of the greatest examples of the spiritual warfare we are up against is found in the book of Daniel. He documents something significant that took place when he was in captivity, serving Cyrus, king of Persia. The Bible says, "In those days I Daniel was mourning three full weeks" (Daniel 10:2).

It seems that Daniel had been fasting, praying, and seeking the Lord for answers regarding his people, Israel.

For nearly three weeks, he heard nothing from God. Then on the twenty-first day he was suddenly visited by an angel clothed in dazzling white linen. In that moment, the Bible says:

> **And, behold, an hand touched me, which set me upon my knees and upon the palms of my hands.**
>
> **And he said unto me, O Daniel, a man greatly beloved, understand the words that I speak unto thee, and stand upright: for unto thee am I now sent. And when he had spoken this word unto me, I stood trembling.**
>
> **Then said he unto me, Fear not, Daniel: for from the first day that thou didst set thine heart to understand, and to chasten thyself before thy God, thy words were heard, and I am come for thy words.**
>
> — Daniel 10:10-12

We see from verse 12 that on the very first day Daniel began to pray, God heard his words, and this heavenly messenger was immediately dispatched to answer Daniel. So why was there a 21-day delay in this divine messenger getting to Daniel? We learn the answer in the next verse:

> **But the prince of the kingdom of Persia withstood me one and twenty days: but, lo, Michael, one of the chief princes, came to help me; and I remained there with the kings of Persia.**
>
> **Now I am come to make thee understand what shall befall thy people in the latter days: for yet the vision is for many days.**
>
> — Daniel 10:13,14

The prince of the kingdom of Persia in verse 13 is a demonic principality that stood over that region, and these verses tell us he came against God's messenger so that he couldn't reach Daniel. He was so strong that the archangel Michael came to help in the fight. Once the angel explained why he had been held up, he began to give Daniel the answers that he needed.

But before then, Daniel had disciplined himself for 21 days, not eating choice foods or drinking wine but only seeking the Lord. During those three weeks, he may have thought God wasn't hearing him or that his prayers weren't being answered. But God had actually sent the answer to Daniel the **first day** he prayed. It was the spiritual opposition that delayed its arrival for 21 days.

Likewise, when we pray, it may be that God has quickly sent the answer, which often, as in this case, is delivered by angelic forces. But they are delayed because of spiritual opposition. By continuing to pray and seeking God's face, we are cooperating with those angelic forces, which are sometimes bursting through spiritual opposition to get us the answers that we need.

Taking New Territory Attracts New Attacks

If you study the Scriptures, you will discover that when the people of Israel were taking new territory in the Promised Land, they came face to face with new attacks. Likewise, when you personally take "new territory" in areas of your life, you too will come up against new waves of spiritual opposition.

For instance, let's say you make a decision to forgive someone for mistreating you. As soon as you begin to walk out that decision, the enemy will often increase his attacks on your mind and emotions, reminding you in vivid detail of what that person said and did to you. As the thoughts and imaginations of how they treated you replay in your mind, you will be tempted to start fighting with that person.

Or maybe you're dealing with sickness or disease that has attacked your body, and you are doing everything you know to do to stand against it. You're praying in faith, quoting God's Word out loud, and guarding your mouth from speaking a negative confession, but nothing seems to be improving. The temptation will be to doubt God's Word, give up on His promises, and draw back from His presence.

Rick shared how one of their faithful employees was working on something that was very important to the ministry, and suddenly a deluge of problems hit him and his family. His wife got sick; his mother broke her arm; and his son was robbed. Needless to say, he was devastated and began asking God, "What in the world is going on?"

If you find yourself facing an overwhelming situation like this, remember the opposition coming against you is not flesh and blood — it is the enemy working behind the scenes trying to get you to quit. This happens to everyone at times, so don't feel defeated if you are dealing with spiritual opposition. Just see it as confirmation that you're on track in your praying — and keep on praying!

Stand Against the *Source* of Your Problems Not the Symptoms

There is one more example of spiritual opposition we want to explore, and it is found in Mark's gospel. It is an event in Scripture that God used to really help Rick through a difficult time many years ago. After a long day of ministry on the shores of the sea of Galilee, Jesus and His disciples got into a boat and set course for the other side. The Bible says:

> **And when they had sent away the multitude, they took him even as he was in the ship. And there were also with him other little ships.**
>
> **And there arose a great storm of wind, and the waves beat into the ship, so that it was now full.**
>
> — Mark 4:36,37

Notice the phrase "there arose" in verse 37. It is a translation of the Greek word *ginomai*, which would be better translated "*suddenly, out of nowhere.*" This word carries the idea of *something unexpected or surprising — the last thing you might think of happening.*

The night that Jesus and His disciples got into the boat and were headed to the other side, there were several disciples on board that were former fishermen who had lived a great deal of their life on those waters. They knew how the currents and the tide behaved, and they were familiar with the weather of that region — including how storms affected the sea.

When they began their journey that night, we know it was a perfect night for sailing, or they would never have gone out on the water. However, when *suddenly, unexpectedly, out of nowhere* "there arose" (the Greek word *ginomai*) a great storm, it took these experienced fishermen totally off guard. It was the last thing they would have expected.

The phrase "storm of wind" in the original text is from a Greek word that describes *turbulence*. And the word "great" is the Greek word *mega*, which means *massive*. Thus, Jesus and His disciples encountered *a massive storm of turbulence*, and while they couldn't see the turbulence, they could certainly feel it. Hence, the sea of Galilee went from calm and peaceful to sudden turbulence, and what they were dealing with was drastic instability that provoked great fear.

It's important to note that the reason Jesus was headed across the lake to the other side was to meet the demoniac of Gadara and cast the legion of demons out of him. His deliverance would result in a great spiritual breakthrough for the whole region (*see* Mark 5:1-20).

Therefore, when the devil saw where Jesus was headed, he attempted to stop Him by suddenly causing a violent windstorm while they were in the middle of the lake. It appeared to come out of nowhere, and it took them completely off guard.

The Bible goes on to say:

> **And he [Jesus] was in the hinder part of the ship, asleep on a pillow: and they awake him, and say unto him, Master, carest thou not that we perish?**
>
> **And he arose, and rebuked the wind, and said unto the sea, Peace, be still. And the wind ceased, and there was a great calm.**
> **— Mark 4:38,39**

It's very important to remember that the disciples had been fighting the waves that kept beating down into the ship (*see* Mark 4:37). They were fighting waves and bailing water, fighting waves and bailing water, again and again. When they were exhausted and couldn't take it any longer, they went to Jesus and said, "Master, don't you even care? We're perishing! You've got to do something about these waves."

What did Jesus deal with when He stood up? It wasn't the waves. It was the *wind* behind the waves. Jesus knew they did not have a wave problem. That was the symptom. That's what they could see. What they had was a *wind* problem that was being generated by the invisible force behind the waves. The disciples could not see it, and they were never going to defeat the wind by fighting the waves. So, when Jesus arose, He rebuked the wind and said to the sea, "Peace, be still." Interestingly, the words "Peace be still" in Greek actually mean "shhh." Jesus told the sea to hush, and it listened!

God Helped Rick Identify and Fight Against the Source of Their Money Problems

Now, the reason this story in Mark 4:35-41 was so important to Rick is because God used it in his life many years ago, when their ministry was having financial struggles that made no sense. Everything was going fine, and the finances were being managed well. But then, suddenly, out of nowhere, the financial giving to the ministry began to dry up.

In his prayers, Rick began to repeatedly tell God, "We need money, God — money, money, money. Help us, Father. Please bring in the money we need to keep everything going."

Rick has jokingly said that people would have thought God's name was money, because every time he raised his hands and his voice in prayer, He would say, "Money, money, money!" Day after day, month after month, he would get out his calculator and work the numbers, fighting and struggling, trying to figure out how to make ends meet.

"I don't understand this," he would tell Denise. "Where did the money go? It just seems like the giving has dried up."

God revealed the real problem. Then one day when Rick approached God with his usual ask for "money, money, money," the Lord spoke to him and said, "You do not have a money problem, Rick."

"What?" Rick responded.

"You do not have a money problem," the Lord said a second time.

"Well, it sure seems to me that we have a money problem," Rick said. "If we don't have a money problem, would You please tell me what kind of problem we have?"

That's when the Lord led Rick to Mark 4 and the story of the disciples fighting the waves. He made it clear to Rick that the disciples didn't have a *wave* problem — they had a *wind* problem. There was an invisible force that was creating all the life-threatening challenges they were dealing with.

As he read through the text, the Holy Spirit told him, "Rick, you do not have a money problem. You have a 'wind' problem. And if you'll quit wrangling with your calculator and deal with the invisible spiritual opposition coming against you, your finances will turn around."

Rick and Denise redirected their prayers. After sharing with Denise what God had revealed to him, they joined hands and prayed together. As they lifted their voices to Heaven, they took authority over the demonic spiritual forces in the unseen realm and began to rebuke them, telling them to cease and to desist their actions.

Then they spoke to their finances and said, "Finances, shhh, be still."

Amazingly, within a matter of days, it was like the financial faucet was turned on again, and the money began to flow into the ministry as it had before. They never had a money problem after that.

As we said earlier, we need to use our head and manage things well with whatever issues we are facing. If you are dealing with financial issues, you need to use your calculator and balance your checkbooks. If you're dealing with a health issue, you need to go to the doctor, take your medication, and do whatever you can. But if none of your efforts in the natural are changing anything, you need to take time to look and see what is working behind the scenes. It may be that there is a spiritual force that you've not taken authority over yet.

Pray for God's discernment and for His proven plan of attack to defeat the opposition against you. Remember, to break through the enemy's resistance, you MUST be committed, because the devil is very committed to stopping you. He will bring discouragement by using others against you or by attacking your mind with thoughts of unbelief. But if you will stay connected with Christ, receive the strength of His Spirit, and stay the course, you will receive the answers you long to receive!

STUDY QUESTIONS

> Study to shew thyself approved unto God, a workman that
> needeth not to be ashamed, rightly dividing the word of truth.
> — 2 Timothy 2:15

1. Take time to slowly reread Daniel 10:1-14 along with First Thessalonians 2:18; Job 1:6,7; 2:1,2; First Peter 5:8; Zechariah 3:1,2;

and Ephesians 6:12. What details is the Holy Spirit highlighting in these passages regarding spiritual opposition? What do you now see that you didn't see before, and how does it help you better understand what you are dealing with?

2. Along with an awareness of the spiritual war we are in, you also need to be aware that the enemy is defeated! Jesus Christ has seized the victory over all the power of the enemy, and as a believer, you share in that victory. In Christ, what is His is also yours! Reflect on these powerful passages and commit them to memory. Then speak them aloud over your life and against the enemy in your times of prayer.

- Colossians 2:15
- Second Corinthians 2:14 and Romans 8:31, 37-39
- First John 4:4; 5:4,5; and John 16:33

3. Although we are in a spiritual war, we are not left powerless. God has armed us with devil-destroying weapons. As a soldier in His army, you need to be aware of what He has given you. Read these verses and identify your spiritual weaponry.

- Ephesians 6:12-18
- Hebrews 4:12; Jeremiah 23:29; and Romans 1:16
- Philippians 2:9-11; Psalm 44:5; John 14:13,14; Acts 3:16; and Mark 16:17,18
- First Peter 1:18,19; Hebrews 10:19; Romans 5:9; First John 1:7; and Revelation 1:5; 12:11

PRACTICAL APPLICATION

> But be ye doers of the word, and not hearers only, deceiving your own selves.
> —James 1:22

1. Carefully reread Rick's candid story of how God showed him the real source of his money problems. What is the Holy Spirit showing you about your own life and the challenges you're facing as you read Rick's testimony? What actions do you sense Him asking you to take?

2. When Jesus stood up to deal with the windstorm, He didn't rebuke the waves — He rebuked the wind. The waves were a *symptom* of the problem; the wind was the *source*. Take a moment to pray: "Lord, what

is the real source of the problem(s) I am dealing with? Is it spiritual opposition in the unseen realm? If so, strengthen me to stand in faith and speak Your Word against the enemy and over my life so that I can see your salvation in my situation. In Jesus' name. Amen!"

LESSON 7

TOPIC

Timing Can Hinder Prayers From Being Answered

SCRIPTURES

1. **Matthew 5:45** — That ye may be the children of your Father which is in heaven: for he maketh his sun to rise on the evil and on the good, and sendeth rain on the just and on the unjust.
2. **Galatians 6:9** — And let us not be weary in well doing: for in due season we shall reap, if we faint not.
3. **James 1:4** — But let patience have her perfect work, that ye may be perfect and entire, wanting nothing.

GREEK WORDS

1. "patience" — ὑπομονή (*hupomone*): to stay or abide; to remain in one's spot; to keep a position; to resolve to maintain territory gained; in a military sense, it pictures soldiers ordered to maintain their positions even in the face of opposition; to defiantly stick it out regardless of pressures mounted against it; staying power; hang-in-there power; the attitude that holds out, holds on, outlasts, perseveres, and hangs in there, never giving up, refusing to surrender to obstacles, and turning down every opportunity to quit; pictures one who is under a heavy load but refuses to bend, break, or surrender because he is convinced that the territory, promise, or principle under assault rightfully belongs to him
2. "perfect" — τέλειος (*teleios*): a word that describes maturity and depicts one graduating from one level up to the next level; thus, when a person stands in faith and exercises trust in God, it causes him to

become spiritually developed and to move into higher levels of spiritual maturity

SYNOPSIS

It can certainly be discouraging to be standing on God's Word — praying and praying and praying for Him to bring something to pass — but nothing is happening. You begin to wonder, *Is God even hearing me? If He is, why isn't He answering me? Am I doing something wrong?*

Thankfully, we serve a merciful God who wants to bless us and wants to answer our prayers. If we will seek Him and ask Him the reason for the delay in answering our prayers, He will show us what to do. He said, "If any of you lacks wisdom, you should ask God, who gives generously to all without finding fault, and it will be given to you" (James 1:5 *NIV*).

In this lesson, we will see that many times the reason that answers to our prayers are delayed or hindered is because it's just not the right time.

The emphasis of this lesson:

God's timing is another crucial factor to receiving answers to our prayers and seeing what He has promised become a reality. We need time between our asking and receiving to grow, mature, and develop the endurance required to manage and fully appreciate the things God has promised.

6 Factors That Influence and Affect Your Prayers

If you are keeping track of what we have covered so far, you know that we have identified six factors that can cause answers to our prayers to be delayed or hindered. Here is a quick list of those factors along with a practical step to overcoming it:

- *Praying inconsistently* — We need God's grace not to waver or vacillate in our prayers.
- *Praying incorrectly* — We need God's grace to know and pray in agreement with His Word.
- *A lack of faith* — To increase our faith, we need to regularly practice hearing God's Word, praying in the Holy Spirit, and exercising our faith.

- *A negative confession* — Getting our heart and mouth into agreement with God's Word yields answers.
- *Bad relationships* — We must let go of unforgiveness to unclog the spiritual pipeline between us and God.
- *Spiritual opposition* — There is an unseen realm in which a real spiritual enemy exists. Although Satan and his minions seek to distract, discourage, and derail us from our God-given destiny, we can overcome them by the strength of the Holy Spirit and by taking authority over them.

As we have noted in each previous lesson, God wants to answer our prayers. In fact, God's desire is to help everyone. Jesus alludes to this in Matthew 5:45, telling us that the Father in Heaven "…maketh his sun to rise on the evil and on the good, and sendeth rain on the just and on the unjust." So, if you haven't received the answer to the prayers you've prayed, there is a reason. And with the help of the Holy Spirit, that reason will be revealed and a plan provided to help you receive what you need from God.

Timing Is Everything

You may have heard it said that anything of value takes time to produce, and that is true. Just ask a farmer and he will tell you. To get a good harvest, it takes time. Once the seeds are planted, the farmer must nurture them by watering the surrounding soil, pulling the weeds, and keeping the pests from damaging the emerging crops.

Rick shared how when he was a boy, he really loved corn, and he decided to grow his own. Although his family lived in the city and he had never done any gardening like that before, there was a little spot along the side of his garage that seemed to be a perfect place. So, he got some seeds, went out with a tiny spatula, and began to dig in the soil and plant his corn kernels. He said:

> I was so careful in the way I planted my seeds. I love for things to be proportional and symmetrical, so I worked hard to make sure the spacing between all the seeds was equal. When I was done, it was nice, neat, and orderly. For a kid in junior high, I did a pretty good job.
>
> When I went out the next day, I expected to see some action. But when I walked up to my little patch of land, there was no activity

at all. A week went by, and there was no change in the garden whatsoever. Day after day, I would come home from school and run to that little piece of land to see if anything was growing, but nothing had changed.

After another week passed and there was still no sign of life, I said, 'There's got to be something wrong with these seeds. They must be defective. They've been in the ground for two weeks, but there's no growth.'

So, I got my same little spatula, and I began to dig up all my seeds to see what was wrong with them. Do you know what I found? My corn seeds had just sprouted roots and were beginning to grow. I dug them up just before they had a chance to pierce through the soil. They weren't defective. They were doing exactly what God designed them to do. Unfortunately, my impatience caused me to dig up my seed and to ruin my harvest."

This story brings to mind what the apostle Paul wrote in Galatians 6:9:

And let us not be weary in well doing: for in due season we shall reap, if we faint not.

"Well-doing" is the things we do to nurture the seeds of faith we have planted in prayer. It includes things like praying the Word over yourself and your situation, standing in faith and not speaking a negative confession, and taking authority over enemy invasion that is trying to steal and sabotage what you are believing God to do.

The fact that the verse says, "And let us not be weary in well-doing," tells us that sometimes we can grow tired of repeatedly doing the right things. When you keep praying and praying and you don't see any results, it can sometimes be very disappointing and exhausting.

Nevertheless, if you stay the course and keep doing and saying and praying what you know is right, the verse goes on to say, "…For in due season we shall reap, if we faint not" (Galatians 6:9). There is a *due season* to everything. In other words, there is a correct, perfect time when all the conditions are right and you are ready to reap what you have been waiting and believing for.

A Practical Example of 'Digging Up Your Seed'

Have you ever known in your heart that God spoke something to you, but you were afraid of seeing it become a reality? That is what Rick experienced in his late teen years when the Holy Spirit revealed to him that Denise was to be his wife. Here is what he candidly shared:

> When I was about 17 years old, I entered college as a freshman, and God began speaking to my heart and to Denise's heart that we were supposed to be married.
>
> At that time, Denise was 22 or 23. Clearly, she was much more mature and advanced than me, and it scared me. Nevertheless, I knew it was God's will for us to get married, so after trying to foster a relationship for only two or three weeks, I made some sort of proposal to her while we were at the ice cream shop.
>
> Surprisingly, she agreed, but as the idea of marriage began to set in, I became terrified and called it off.
>
> 'Denise,' I said, 'This is not God's will. We need to call it off.'
>
> 'Well, okay,' she responded bewilderedly. At that point, Denise really didn't know me, and what she did know about me — like the fact that I had a pet snake — made her think I was a bit strange, which I could understand.
>
> Nearly two years went by, and in fear, I was still holding to the notion that getting married was now *not* God's will. Ironically, at the same time, I was also putting notes on Denise's car and calling to talk with her, which made me appear even stranger in her eyes.
>
> Then suddenly, I had a change of heart, and I proposed to Denise again. This time, I attempted to be real spiritual about it, telling her, 'I want to love you as Christ loves the Church, and I'm asking you to be my wife.'
>
> Keep in mind, we had hardly talked for two years, so we had no relationship. Because she was an older, more mature woman, the idea of moving forward in marriage scared the living daylights out of me. That was why I called off marriage the first time and

tried to run away from her, but I couldn't stay away. I knew in my heart God wanted us to be together.

Now, when I proposed to Denise the second time, we were having breakfast together. Of course, she cried and was deeply moved when I popped the question. But this time, instead of simply answering yes, she looked at me and said, 'Rick, if you and I were just spirits, we could get married tomorrow. But we're not just spirits — we're much more complex beings.'

Amazingly, that was her answer to my proposal, which I didn't quite understand. At any rate, we finished our breakfast and went our separate ways. I called her a few times and went to see her once. Then I disappeared for a while.

What is with this guy? Denise thought. *He proposes, calls it off for two years, proposes again, and then disappears. I just don't understand him.*

I didn't know it then, but looking back, I can see that the will of God for Denise and me to be married was planted in my heart, but the timing for it to sprout up and come to life was not right. Each time I took back my proposal and disappeared was like me digging up my corn seeds to see what was happening.

The fact is that I had to grow up and mature in order to marry Denise. The decision to get married was correct, but I was out of God's timing. I am so grateful we didn't get married when I was 17. That would have been disastrous.

Time passed, and God showed me that my running away from Denise was disobedience. So, I began to pursue her once again. Eventually, I proposed a third time, and it stuck! We became husband and wife, and now, more than four decades later, we are living the dream God put in our heart. As He says in His Word: 'He has made everything beautiful in its time…' (Ecclesiastes 3:11 *NKJV*).

We Need Time To Be Prepared for What God Has Prepared for Us

Shortly after Rick and Denise were married, the Holy Spirit began to speak to Rick and give him a vision for the ministry he would oversee. In that vision, the Lord showed him that he and Denise would start a church, and from that church a number of affiliate churches would be born and scattered all around it.

Time passed, and Rick continued to pray about the vision. It soon became so strong in his heart that one day he turned to Denise and said, "It's time! We're going to do it." Accordingly, they launched out and planted a church.

Unfortunately, what they did was not God's will, and the ministry quickly turned into a total failure, leaving Rick, Denise, and their young family financially destitute. Thankfully, God mercifully got through to Rick that he was in error, and he closed the church and got back on track with the Lord's plan for their lives.

Make no mistake: the vision Rick saw was from God, and it was correct. His timing was just off.

Today, he and Denise oversee a central church in Moscow, Russia, called the Moscow Good News Church, and it is surrounded by numerous affiliate campuses. What he saw more than four decades earlier did come to pass. But it would take nearly 35 years before the time was right for it to fully manifest.

Sometimes God does indeed speak something to us, and when it doesn't happen for a long time, we get discouraged. In such cases, the hindrance is not that we've prayed wrong or even that we are experiencing spiritual opposition.

The issue is that God is waiting for us to grow up and have enough maturity in our character so that we can handle what He wants to give us. Thus, the issue is timing.

Time Is Needed To Develop Endurance

This brings us to a very important verse, which is applicable to prayer. Writing under the inspiration of the Holy Spirit, James said:

> **But let patience have her perfect work, that ye may be perfect and entire, wanting nothing.**
> —James 1:4

Please take note of the word "patience." It is a translation of the remarkable Greek word *hupomone*, which means *to stay or abide*, *to remain in one's spot*, *to keep a position*, or *to resolve to maintain territory gained*. In a military sense, it pictures soldiers ordered to maintain their positions even in the face of opposition.

This word *hupomone* carries the idea of one who defiantly sticks it out regardless of pressures mounted against him. It could also be translated as *staying power* or *hang-in-there power*. It is the attitude that holds out, holds on, outlasts, perseveres, and hangs in there, never giving up, refusing to surrender to obstacles, and turning down every opportunity to quit.

Moreover, it pictures one who is under a heavy load but refuses to bend, break, or surrender because he is convinced that the territory, promise, or principle under assault rightfully belongs to him.

This verse in James lets us know that we need time to allow patience to *have her perfect work*. That word "perfect" is a form of the Greek word *teleios*, a term that describes *maturity* and depicts *one graduating from one level up to the next level*. Thus, when a person stands in faith and exercises trust in God, it causes him to become spiritually developed and to move into higher levels of spiritual maturity.

Oftentimes, maturity is required before you can receive the manifestation of what God promised. If you will cooperate with the Holy Spirit and let patience (*hupomone*) have its perfect work, you will mature and be promoted into the new thing God has called you to do. Just as He was waiting on Rick to mature so he could finally marry Denise, it may be that He is waiting for you to grow up so you can receive the manifestation of what He promised.

When we factor in the original Greek meaning of the key words in this verse, the *Renner Interpretive Version* (*RIV*) of James 1:4 is as follows:

> But you're the one that must make the choice to let this God-given endurance do its work. And if you'll let endurance run its full course, it will advance you into higher levels of spiritual maturity. Choosing to let endurance run its full course takes work — but if you'll stick with this process all the way to the end, you'll advance to high spiritual levels in your life. Not only that, but you'll have in your possession the quality necessary to possess your God-given inheritance — ending up with

no deficits, shortages, or lack of any kind, and I mean none whatsoever.

Sometimes Unanswered Prayers Are a Blessing in Disguise

If you really stop and think about it, if God had given you many of the things you asked for right when you prayed for them, you would have lost them because you didn't have the maturity to handle them. Even though your vision from God was correct and your asking was accurate, the timing was not right.

More than likely, some of the things you prayed for years ago you are about to see come to pass in your life in the days ahead. Today, because of all the experiences you now have, you are not the same person you were when you first prayed. You are different. The timing is now right, and you are prepared for what God has prepared for you.

In addition to our need to mature, we also need time between our asking and receiving so that we can truly appreciate what God gives us. Have you ever watched someone get something and be ungrateful for it? It is not a pretty sight. God loves us enough to allow for time in the equation so that when we finally receive what He has promised, we truly appreciate, value, and treasure it as a gift. With this attitude of gratitude, we can also receive the full benefits of the blessing.

Keep in mind, there are some things God gives us instantly. For example, salvation comes to anyone the moment they ask God for forgiveness and invite Jesus into their life. Peace of mind and freedom from worry and fear also come instantaneously when we ask. Likewise, deliverance and healing are often granted the instant we ask.

But asking God for a big ministry or the huge business in your field is not likely a request He is going to answer immediately. Yes, it may very well be the will of God that you oversee a large ministry or have the biggest business in town, but if you are not mature enough to handle it, He loves you too much to give it to you immediately. You need patience to run its perfect course first so that you will be able to handle everything that comes with the promotion.

Are You 'Pregnant' With a Promise From God?

When a woman gets pregnant, she doesn't give birth the next day. Can you imagine a baby going from conception to infant size in 24 hours? That would be horrific for the mother and the child. For example, in the woman's body alone, time is needed to accommodate for the countless changes, such as changes in hormone levels, development of the placenta, expansion of the womb, not to mention mental and emotional adjustments.

A mere 24 hours is too fast to conceive and receive a baby. It takes time.

Then there is the practical side of preparation. You need time to get a room ready for a baby — time to clean, decorate, and furnish the new space for the new life that is coming. Thank God He gives us about nine months before the child's arrival because we need that time to prepare on all levels, including mentally, emotionally, and relationally.

In the same way that pregnancy must run its full course before a mother delivers her baby, when you are pregnant with a promise from God, the stages of development must run their full course before that dream is delivered. Babies born prematurely can often develop challenges that threaten their survival. The same can happen to a dream birthed outside of God's timing. What seems like an unwanted delay to your prayers being answered can be a necessary season of growth, preparation, and development.

The prayer is right. What you see is right. What you believe is right. But you're in the middle of the process. And rather than just wring your hands and say, "It's not working. It's not working." Why don't you say, "God help me do what I need to do and change how I need to change so I can accommodate the answer and receive it."

Focus on personal growth so you can receive what Jesus wants to give you. And when you reach that point, *bam!*, that answer is going to come through that prayer conduit and you're going to receive the answer to your prayer.

STUDY QUESTIONS

Study to shew thyself approved unto God, a workman that needeth not to be ashamed, rightly dividing the word of truth.
— 2 Timothy 2:15

1. Who can you think of in the Bible that God made a promise to or gave a dream to who then had to wait a long time for it to become a reality? Consider the lives of Abraham (*see* Genesis 12-25); Joseph (*see* Genesis 37-50); and David (*see* 1 Samuel 16-31; 2 Samuel 1-2). A study of these men will help you better understand the process of God's timing and what happens in us while we wait.

2. Rick shared how God spoke to his heart about marrying Denise and also gave him a vision for the ministry he would one day oversee. What has God spoken to *you*? What vision has He placed in your heart about *your life* that you are still waiting to be fulfilled? Take a few moments to write down what you believe He has promised.

PRACTICAL APPLICATION

But be ye doers of the word, and not hearers only, deceiving your own selves.
— James 1:22

1. Think for a moment. What if God answered every prayer you prayed right when you prayed it? How do you think that would turn out? Looking back over your life, are there any prayers you are grateful God didn't answer? If so, which one(s)? How was the unanswered prayer a blessing?

2. What is one thing you know God promised and spoke to your heart, but you had to pray, wait, and trust Him to bring it about? In what areas of your life did you need time to grow and mature so that you would be ready to receive the blessing He had for you?

3. The fact that the Bible says, "And let us not be weary in well-doing," tells us that sometimes we can grow tired of repeatedly doing the right things. Is that where you are? Are you emotionally and mentally spent from doing the right things but seeing no results? Pray and ask the Lord to *infuse you with new strength and hope* to continue to trust Him until He brings to pass what He has promised. As you pray,

reflect on His promises in Isaiah 40:28-31; 41:10; Acts 1:8; Second Corinthians 12:9,10; and Philippians 4:13.

LESSON 8

TOPIC
Sin May Affect Your Prayers Being Answered

SCRIPTURES
1. **Matthew 5:45** — That ye may be the children of your Father which is in heaven: for he maketh his sun to rise on the evil and on the good, and sendeth rain on the just and on the unjust.
2. **Psalm 66:18** — If I regard iniquity in my heart, the Lord will not hear me.
3. **1 John 1:9** — If we confess our sins, he is faithful and just to forgive us our sins, and to cleanse us from all unrighteousness.

GREEK WORDS
No Greek words were shown on the TV program.

SYNOPSIS
Once more, we turn our attention to our anchor verse in Matthew 5:45, where Jesus says that our Father in Heaven "…maketh his sun to rise on the evil and on the good, and sendeth rain on the just and on the unjust." This passage tells us plainly that God wants to bless and help everyone — it's His nature. However, there are sometimes things that prevent Him from answering our prayers.

Probably the most obvious reason for God not answering our prayers is because there is *sin* in our life that we have not addressed. The prophet Isaiah pointed this out to the people of Israel, telling them, "Listen now! The Lord isn't too weak to save you. And he isn't getting deaf! He can hear you when you call! But the trouble is that your sins have cut you off from God. Because of sin he has turned his face away from you and will not listen…" (Isaiah 59:1,2 *TLB*).

Thankfully, there is a remedy for all sin! The Bible says, "If we confess our sins, he is faithful and just to forgive us our sins, and to cleanse us from all unrighteousness" (1 John 1:9). Praise God for His rich, unearnable mercy and faithfulness to forgive our sins and make us clean again!

The emphasis of this lesson:

God calls intentional sin that we coddle in our heart iniquity, and when we allow this kind of sin to remain unchecked in our lives, it hinders our prayers. Coming clean and confessing our sins to God is what reopens His ears to hear and answer our prayers.

8 Factors That Influence and Affect Your Prayers

So far in this series, we have examined seven factors that can cause answers to our prayers to be hindered. Here is a quick review of what those factors are:

1. *Praying inconsistently* — Our prayers become a moving target, making it hard for God to answer us because we keep wavering in our faith.
2. *Praying incorrectly* — This is "praying amiss" (*see* James 4:3), which is not praying according to Scripture.
3. *A lack of faith* — This condition results from focusing on and talking about our problem rather than focusing on and filling ourselves with the truth of God's Word.
4. *A negative confession* — Speaking doubtful, negative things will nullify the prayers of faith we have prayed.
5. *Bad relationships* — When we hold on to unforgiveness toward those who hurt us, bitterness builds in our hearts and blocks God's answers from reaching us.
6. *Spiritual opposition* — We're in a war against an unseen but very real enemy, and if we don't take authority over him and his imps, they can keep us from receiving what God has for us.
7. *Timing* — To experience the dreams and promises God has put in our hearts, we need time to grow and mature so that we can handle and fully appreciate them.

The *eighth* factor that can cause answers to our prayers to be delayed or hindered is having *sin* in our lives. Specifically, this is a known, intentional, blatant sin that we allow to remain in our lives unrestrained. It is sin that the Bible often refers to as *iniquity*, and it deeply grieves the heart of God.

We Are Not to 'Regard Iniquity' in Our Heart

One of the scriptures that addresses this issue of "iniquity" is Psalm 66:18, which says, "If I regard *iniquity* in my heart, the Lord will not hear me." Now, all of us commit sin at times — many times we're not even aware of it. This would include having a bad attitude toward others or toward a task we have been asked to do. Other times, we commit sins of *omission*, which means we *omit*, or *fail to do*, something that we should have done.

When we sin in these ways, it does not mean God will no longer hear us. That is not what Psalm 66:18 is talking about. "Regarding iniquity in our heart" is not something we accidentally do — it is sin we do deliberately.

In this passage, the word "regard" in the original language means *I see* or *I imagine*. Therefore, we could translate Psalm 66:18 to say, "If *I see* or if *I imagine* iniquity in my heart, the Lord will not hear me." Here the psalmist is talking about pondering, fantasizing, and conceiving sin in your heart. In other words, you are imagining and meditating on things in your heart that you know are wrong. This is the "iniquity" — or intentional sin — that can block the Lord from hearing you.

An example of this kind of sin would be holding on to unforgiveness in your heart toward someone who has hurt you. Instead of being willing to forgive and release the person into God's hands, you refuse to forgive and choose to hold on to their offense, replaying what they did or said over and over until unforgiveness turns into bitterness, resentment, and even hatred.

To "regard iniquity in your heart" is to keep that wrong thing alive inside you. You keep seeing it and hearing it in your soul, and the more you allow the thoughts and images to percolate inside you, the stronger it grows. Psalm 66:18 calls this deliberate action iniquity (sin), and if you do this, it will shut God's ears to your prayers.

Thankfully, you can reopen His ears to your prayers by *repenting*. In the case of unforgiveness, a prayer of repentance might include you saying,

"Lord, please forgive me for holding on to unforgiveness toward this person. You are the Judge, not me, and You have forgiven me of countless things. Therefore, I choose to forgive this person and release them into Your hands. Please heal the hurt they have caused and help me forgive them. In Jesus' name. Amen."

Complaining and Murmuring Is a Form of Iniquity

Another example of "regarding iniquity in our heart" is *complaining*. Surprisingly, many Christians practice this form of negativity and don't even see it as a problem. Nevertheless, it is most definitely a problem, because it clogs the pipeline of prayer between us and God. Complaining is so infectious that the Lord commands us in Philippians 2:14:

Do all things without murmuring and disputing.

Interestingly, the word "disputing" means *murmuring* in the Greek. To murmur is to *mutter things in low tones under one's breath*. The *Amplified Classic* version of Philippians 2:14 really makes this clear, telling us:

Do all things without grumbling and faultfinding and complaining [against God] and questioning and doubting [among yourselves].

If you think about it, when you complain and murmur, it is usually about people. It's as if you are seeing and hearing certain individuals inside your soul, and the memory of the things they do that you don't like plays like a movie on the screen of your heart.

Although some of us have been able not to complain out loud, we are still complaining in our heart. You might even say murmuring and complaining is taking up real estate inside us.

We keep it alive in our mind by thinking things like…

- *Oh, I can't stand it when they do [fill in the blank]. Who do they think that they are?*
- *Here we go again… This kind of stuff always happens to me.*
- *I'm so sick and tired of all this!*
- *If they do that one more time, I'm just going to scream!*

Now if you have ever been around someone who complains all the time, the thing you want most of all is to get away from them. In addition to being annoying and exhausting, their words are also hurtful and harmful. On the other hand, those who do *not* complain are *harmless* — the Bible says so. You can see it for yourself when we read Philippians 2:14 and 15 together:

> **Do all things without murmurings and disputings: That ye may be blameless and harmless, the sons of God, without rebuke, in the midst of a crooked and perverse nation, among whom ye shine as lights in the world.**

This passage tells us that the person who, by the grace of God, chooses not to complain and murmur has the presence and power of God in their life, and it is so significant that they "shine as lights in the world."

Make no mistake: God is fully aware of where we live and all the negative influences that are around us. He knows that we could very easily murmur and complain, but He commands us not to so that we become a harmless and blameless beacon of His light in the midst of our crooked and perverse culture.

Remember, Jesus said, "…Out of the abundance of the heart the mouth speaketh" (Matthew 12:34). Isn't it interesting that people who are truly happy in their heart never complain? Only depressed people complain. Likewise, a complaining person is never thankful, and a thankful person is never complaining. Lord, please help us develop an attitude of gratitude from the inside out and rid ourselves of all murmuring and complaining, in Jesus' name!

Sins of the Attitude Can Be Very Detrimental to Our Prayers

Now when most people think about regarding iniquity in their heart, they often think it refers to things like sexual temptation or premeditated murder, because "regarding iniquity" means *to see, to imagine, to meditate on,* or *to fantasize* things in one's heart that are knowingly wrong.

Without question, premeditated murder is regarding iniquity. The very word "premeditated" means *to think about and meditate on in advance* or before actually doing the action — which in this case is murder. Someone who commits premeditated murder has visualized and imagined carrying out their heinous act countless times before they go through with it.

Likewise, the practice of looking at pornography is a serious form of sin. If a person is looking at porn or tempted sexually with lustful thoughts toward others, he or she is imagining it and seeing it in their heart. Hence, it is regarding iniquity, and anyone involved in such behavior should repent and make every effort to break free from it. There are special programs for your computer that will block those images and videos from entering your home. Likewise, there are things you can install on your phone to help prevent porn from popping up.

But these are really extreme examples. The fact is that there are other sins — especially sins of the attitude — that are equally as wrong. Complaining, murmuring, unforgiveness, resentment, bitterness, gossip, and slander all fall into this category, and they affect everyone. Although many people think these things are not that bad, they are. When we tolerate and entertain them in our heart, it is regarding iniquity, and the Bible says, "...The Lord will not hear me" (Psalm 66:18).

These sins clog the spiritual pipeline between us and God, causing Him to close His ears to us and hindering us from hearing Him. It's very hard to receive anything from God when we have these kinds of things at work in our soul taking up real estate. We can't hear from Him because we already have our own theater playing inside us.

Confessing Our Sins Reopens God's Ears to Our Prayers

If we were to stop right there, we would be most miserable, because all of us have sinned and fallen short of the glory of God (*see* Romans 3:23). Thankfully, there is something that reopens the Father's ears to our prayers, and it is found in First John 1:9, which says:

> **If we confess our sins, he is faithful and just to forgive us our sins, and to cleanse us from all unrighteousness.**

Notice the word "confess." It is a translation of the Greek word *homologian*, which can be translated *to confess* or *to agree with*. It's not just you saying, "God, I confess my sin," and then you're done. It's you and God getting into alignment and getting on the same page on the issue.

To confess your sins is to get alone with God and say, "All right, God. I know what You say about this in Your Word, and I'm wrong. I'm not going to hide it anymore. I'm going to agree with You. I say what You say about my behavior and about my attitude. I will no longer call it a mistake or my weakness. I'm going to call it what You call it. My attitude and my behavior are sin — period. It is wrong, offensive, and it closes Your ears to me. I'm confessing it for what it is."

Very often, a confession like this doesn't take place in a matter of seconds. Instead, it might require spending longer time with God and just really getting honest with Him. But if you will sincerely confess your sins, getting into agreement and on the same page with Him concerning what you did wrong, "…He is faithful and just to forgive us our sins, and to cleanse us from all unrighteousness" (1 John 1:9).

God 'Forgives' and 'Cleanses' Us From All Unrighteousness

Another very important word in First John 1:9 is the word "forgive," which is a form of the Greek word *aphiemi*, and it means *to release and to let it go*. In today's culture, people often say, "Just let it go," and that is what the word "forgiveness" means. Therefore, when we cry out to God from our heart and say, "Father, I'm getting on the same page with You about what I've done. It's sin, and I'm asking You for Your help. Please forgive me and cleanse me with the blood of Jesus," He hears and forgives.

When you confess your sins, God literally says, "You know what? I'm going to release that sin from you — I'm just going to let it go." But that's not all He does. It just so happens that the word *aphiemi* — translated here as "forgive" — also means *to send so far away that you can never reach over to retrieve it and pull it back to bring it up again*. It is permanently dismissed, sent away forever. That is exactly what David wrote in Psalm 103:12:

> **As far as the east is from the west, so far hath he removed our transgressions from us.**

When God forgives your sins, you are totally liberated! In that renewed position, suddenly His ears are wide open to hear you pray again.

And along with forgiving you, First John 1:9 says God will *cleanse* you from all unrighteousness. The word "cleanse" here is a form of the Greek word *katharidzo*, which is where we get our medical term for a *catheter*.

When a person is in the hospital, he or she can't get up and go to the bathroom. So, the nurses insert a catheter into the patient to release all the fluids from their bladder. All the toxins from the body flow through this very small tube, out of the body, and into a storage bag. This is how your body is *cleansed*.

Spiritually speaking, when you get on the same page with God and confess your sins, He doesn't just release them and let them go. He places a spiritual catheter in you and drains all the foul, poisonous things that you've been regarding in your heart. That is the kind of complete cleansing He provides through the blood of Jesus!

STUDY QUESTIONS

Study to shew thyself approved unto God, a workman that needeth not to be ashamed, rightly dividing the word of truth.
— 2 Timothy 2:15

1. Take a few moments to look up Numbers 32:23; Proverbs 26:26; Ecclesiastes 12:14; Luke 12:2; and First Corinthians 4:5. What sobering truth is repeated in all these verses?

2. As a believer, harboring sin in your heart never produces good results. King David held on to his sins and attempted to keep them covered for quite some time. What was the outcome of "regarding iniquity in his heart"? Carefully read what he wrote in Psalm 32 and identify what happened when he kept silent and then when he confessed his sin. What advice does he give to you and all God's people about coming clean with the Lord about what is in your heart?

3. One of the best ways to keep iniquity (sin) from lodging and growing in your heart is — to the best of your ability — avoid the people, places, and things that you know trip you up and seem to suck you into sin. That is what the Bible tells us, and these two passages really make this clear:

Let your way in life be far from her (*sin*), and come not near the door of her house [avoid the very scenes of temptation] (Proverbs 5:8 *AMPC*).

Therefore then, since we are surrounded by so great a cloud of witnesses [who have borne testimony to the Truth], let us strip off and throw aside every encumbrance (unnecessary weight) and that

sin which so readily (deftly and cleverly) clings to and entangles us, and let us run with patient endurance and steady and active persistence the appointed course of the race that is set before us, looking away [from all that will distract] to Jesus, Who is the Leader and the Source of our faith… (Hebrews 12:1,2 *AMPC*).

What is the Holy Spirit showing you in these passages about sin, temptation, and your own life? What specific "scenes of temptation" do you know you need to avoid? What sin *readily and cleverly clings to and entangles* you that you need to strip off?

Start your prayer time every morning by getting quiet and asking the Holy Spirit to show you if there is anything that you need to repent of (*see* Psalm 139:23,24); if He reveals something to you, then repent and obey what He tells you. Also, ask Him for grace (strength) to live right (*see* James 4:6).

PRACTICAL APPLICATION

> But be ye doers of the word, and not hearers only, deceiving your own selves.
> —James 1:22

1. "Regarding iniquity in our heart" is not a sin we commit accidentally — it is sin we do deliberately. In all honesty, are you involved in any kind of deliberate, intentional sin? Are you seeing, imagining, or pondering things in your heart that you know are wrong and not repenting and working with the Holy Spirit to overcome it?
2. When you hear the words *murmuring* and *complaining*, what person comes to mind? In contrast, who do you know, as a rule, that does *not* complain or murmur? How would you describe the overall state of each of these people's lives? In which category would those closest to you place you?
3. If you have felt like God's ears have been closed to your prayers, you need to get alone in His presence and ask if there's anything sinful you've been entertaining in your heart, such as bad attitudes of complaining, unforgiveness, bitterness, resentment, gossip, or slander. If the Holy Spirit shows you something wrong, agree with Him and confess it as sin.

LESSON 9

TOPIC
What To Do if Answers to Your Prayers Are Delayed or Hindered, Part 1

SCRIPTURES
Colossians 4:2 — Continue in prayer, and watch in the same with thanksgiving.

GREEK WORDS

1. "continue" — **προσκαρτερέω** (*proskartereo*): a strong, solid, never-give-up type of leaning toward an object; pictures one who desires something so passionately that he is pressing toward it; one so devoted to obtaining something that he is busily engaged in activities that will eventually bring it to him

2. "prayer" — **προσευχή** (*proseuche*): close, up-front, intimate contact; coming close to express a wish, desire, prayer, or vow; used to depict a person who vowed to give something of great value to God in exchange for a favorable answer to prayer; it portrays an individual who desires to see his prayer answered so desperately that he is willing to surrender everything he owns in exchange for answered prayer; hence, contained in this word is the concept of surrender

3. "watch" — **γρηγορέω** (*gregoreo*): depicts a person whose attitude is to never let up; to be watchful; to be wide awake; one who is not asleep on the job

4. "thanksgiving" — **εὐχαριστία** (*eucharistia*): an outpouring of a heart full of grace, gratitude, and feelings that freely flow from the heart in response to someone or something

SYNOPSIS

According to God's Word, our prayers are powerful! James 5:16 (*AMPC*) declares, "…The earnest (heartfelt, continued) prayer of a righteous man makes tremendous power available [dynamic in its working]." With our prayers, we communicate with God — we talk to Him and He talks to us.

But what are we to do when we just can't seem to get through? When our prayers appear to be bouncing off the ceiling and going unanswered? Clearly, there are certain conditions that affect whether our prayers are answered. So far, we have carefully examined eight factors that can delay or hinder our prayers, and they are:

1) Praying Inconsistently

2) Praying Incorrectly

3) A Lack of Faith

4) A Negative Confession

5) Bad Relationships

6) Spiritual Opposition

7) Timing

8) Sin

Now, you may be saying, "To the best of my ability, I have dealt with all eight of these factors and am doing everything right. But I still am not getting answers to my prayers. What should I do?" Getting angry with God or yourself won't help, and throwing in the towel and quitting is just what the devil wants. Thankfully, there is another option that is biblical and proven to be effective, and that will be our focus in this lesson.

The emphasis of this lesson:

Once you've dealt with the eight factors that can delay and hinder our prayers, God instructs you to continue in prayer, which means to keep pressing forward through any obstacles and into the Holy Spirit, His Word, and prayer until you finally receive what you have been after. As you press forward, stay wide awake and thank God in advance for the answer.

'Continue in Prayer'

If you have done everything you know to do and dealt with the eight common obstacles to unanswered prayer — and are still not seeing results — the next step is to do what Paul said in Colossians 4:2:

> **Continue in prayer, and watch in the same with thanksgiving.**

That's the answer — *continue in prayer*. Although on the surface this might sound flippant, it is not. There is great meaning in this word "continue," which is a translation of the Greek word *proskartereo*. It describes *a strong, solid, never-give-up type of leaning toward an object*. It pictures one who desires something so passionately that he is pressing toward it. Moreover, it is one so devoted to obtaining something that he is busily engaged in activities that will eventually bring it to him.

So, when Paul writes, "Continue in prayer…," he is instructing and urging us to keep pressing forward in prayer. Keep pressing into the Spirit, pressing into God's Word, and pressing into prayer until you finally receive what you have been after. That's what the word "continue" means here.

As you keep pressing into the Holy Spirit, ask Him to show you if you are facing spiritual opposition or if there is another factor you may have missed. He will reveal what is happening. Whatever you do, don't give up! If you keep pressing forward in prayer and refuse to give up, you will outlast the enemy and obtain what you are praying for. And when the test is over, you will emerge on the other side of it more mature and ready for what God has ready for you.

What Are Some of the Things We Need To Press Through?

To *continue in prayer*, you must develop an unstoppable attitude and press forward through things that are blocking your way to receiving what you need. Although the list of obstacles is seemingly endless, here are a few of the major ones:

Offense is a huge barrier to the breakthrough you are looking for. When you hold on to the hurt that others have inflicted, *unforgiveness* begins to build in your heart. If you don't deal with it, it turns into what the Bible calls a root of *bitterness*, and if bitterness is not addressed, it becomes *resentment* and eventually *hatred*. Dealing with offense starts with you lining your will up with God and saying, "Lord, *I want to want* to forgive this person. With Your grace, I choose to release them and forgive them." This begins the process of pressing through offense and unforgiveness, and it continues with praying for those who hurt you to be blessed (*see* 1 Peter 3:8-12).

Fear is another major factor that can prevent you from moving forward into what God has for you. Anxiety and worry are the most common forms of fear that come against you, not to mention the fear of what people are thinking and saying about you. The Bible says, "The fear of man brings a snare, but whoever leans on, trusts in, and puts his confidence in the Lord is safe and set on high" (Proverbs 29:25 *AMPC*). Whenever you feel anxious, worried, or afraid of anything, seek the Lord and cast all those fears and concerns on Him. Like David, you will come to say, "I sought the Lord, and he heard me, and delivered me from all my fears" (Psalm 34:4).

Doubt is yet another barrier you must purposely press through. When you've been praying and praying for something to come to pass for a long time, the enemy will slither in and try to ransack you with doubt. He'll whisper things like, "You've been praying about this long enough, and it still hasn't happened. Just cut it out. If God was going to do it, He would have done it by now. Stop wasting your time and energy and just walk away." When doubt comes, remember Jesus' words and push passed it. He said, "…Whosoever shall say unto this mountain, Be thou removed, and be thou cast into the sea; and *shall not doubt* in his heart, but *shall believe* that those things which he saith shall come to pass; he shall have whatsoever he saith" (Mark 11:23).

Your flesh itself is probably the greatest obstacle that you need to press through. Rick shared how, when he was being interviewed on a TV program, he was asked what the worst enemy was that he had to overcome. Of course, the interviewer was waiting for some big, deep, mysterious answer. So you can imagine the shock when Rick looked into the camera and said, "Me! My flesh is the worst enemy I have had to overcome."

Let's face it, sometimes you are just lazy or tired and you want to give up. But you can't let your flesh — which is basically the desires of your body and soul (mind, will, and emotions) — call the shots. You have to press through. That is what Jesus did. He was in the Garden of Gethsemane, going through the worst moment of His life, and the Spirit of God in Him was wrestling with His human flesh. He could have called legions of angels from Heaven to come and deliver Him, but He didn't. Instead, He pressed through the desires of His flesh and prayed, "…Nevertheless not my will, but thine, be done" (Luke 22:42). He then did what He had been sent to do — He paid the penalty for our sin, sacrificing His very life to redeem us from sin and Satan's power.

Remember, your spirit is willing, but your flesh is weak. Pressing through in prayer will enable you to win out against your flesh and accomplish God's purposes.

God's People — Then and Now — Have To Press Through Many Challenges

As you study the Scriptures, you will see that every person, man or woman, who did something for God with their lives had to press through difficult things. The most obvious example in the New Testament is the apostle Paul. When his character came into question among the believers at the church in Corinth, he pressed through their accusations and gave them a brief overview of what he had endured:

> **Of the Jews five times received I forty stripes save one.**
>
> **Thrice was I beaten with rods, once was I stoned, thrice I suffered shipwreck, a night and a day I have been in the deep;**
>
> **In journeyings often, in perils of waters, in perils of robbers, in perils by mine own countrymen, in perils by the heathen, in perils in the city, in perils in the wilderness, in perils in the sea, in perils among false brethren;**
>
> **In weariness and painfulness, in watchings often, in hunger and thirst, in fastings often, in cold and nakedness.**
> — **2 Corinthians 11:24-27**

Clearly, it was not a piece of cake for Paul to endure all the challenges he went through. He could have died numerous times, but God preserved his life through it all. With a sincere, driving desire to intimately know Christ, Paul said, "…This one thing I do, forgetting those things which are behind, and reaching forth unto those things which are before, I *press* toward the mark for the prize of the high calling of God in Christ Jesus" (Philippians 3:13,14).

Many of the people you see who are succeeding and making a difference for Christ often have a backstory filled with trials and challenges of which you are not aware. Take Rick and Denise, for example. In their autobiography *Unlikely*, they candidly share shocking stories of what they've experienced, including unimaginable mistreatment, harsh conditions, government sanctions, and being lied about by other Christians in ministry. Clearly, they've had multiple opportunities along the way to quit, but they stayed the course. With the strength of God, they have pressed through like Paul, and God has preserved them. And they are still actively doing the will of God today.

'Prayer' Is a Place of Surrender and Exchange

Looking again at Colossians 4:2, Paul said we are to "Continue in prayer...." The word "prayer" here is a form of the Greek word *proseuche*, which describes *close*, *up-front*, *intimate contact*. It carries the idea of coming close to express a wish, desire, prayer, or vow. This word *proseuche* was used to depict a person who vowed to give something of great value to God in exchange for a favorable answer to prayer. In fact, this individual so desperately desires to see his prayer answered that he is willing to surrender everything he owns in exchange for answered prayer. Hence, contained in this word *proseuche* — translated here as "prayer" — is the concept of *surrender*.

What's interesting is that the second part of this word — *euche* — describes *a votive offering*. In the ancient world, when someone needed a favorable answer from the gods, they would come to an altar and make a deal with that god. They would say, "I'm going to give this to you (god), in exchange for something that you will give to me." Thus, *proseuche* was a place of exchange where someone made a vow and was willing to surrender something for a favorable answer.

The word *proseuche* is the most often translated word for "prayer" in the entire New Testament, which means **prayer is most often a place of surrender and prayer is a place of exchange.**

One of the best examples of the use of this word *proseuche* (prayer) in the entire Bible is in First Samuel 1, where we read about a Hebrew woman named Hannah who was barren. At that time, there was a societal stigma that she felt because she was childless. So, year after year, she would journey to Shiloh with her husband, Elkanah, to worship God and make sacrifices to Him, and when she came, she would pray earnestly, asking Him to give her a child.

Finally, one year when she came and was pouring out her heart to God, she came to a place of *proseuche* where she was no longer just asking Him for something, but she was willing to make an exchange and surrender something to Him. She said:

> **…O Lord of hosts, if thou wilt indeed look on the affliction of thine handmaid, and remember me, and not forget thine handmaid, but wilt give unto thine handmaid a man child, then I will give him unto the Lord all the days of his life, and there shall no razor come upon his head.**
>
> **— 1 Samuel 1:11**

That's what God was waiting for — Hannah to come to a place of full surrender. When she did, God opened her womb and she conceived a son, and his name was Samuel. Once the boy was weaned, Hannah fulfilled her vow to the Lord and surrendered Samuel into His hands. Eli the priest would oversee his life and train him up in the Lord's service.

Because Hannah was faithful to her promise, "The Lord visited Hannah, so that she conceived, and bare three sons and two daughters…" (1 Samuel 2:21).

Are You Waiting on God or Is God Waiting on You?

Sometimes as we are continuing to press in, God is wanting us to come to a place of prayer where we say, "All right, Lord, is there anything in me that's stopping me from receiving from You? If so, what is it? What do I need to give up, place in Your hands, and walk away from so I can receive from You?"

When you come to that place of surrender and you're willing to exchange something with God to receive what you need, very often, that's when He responds very quickly, and He releases what you've been pressing and pressing forward to receive.

The fact is, there are often issues in our life that block the answers to our prayers. But when we draw close to God in prayer, the Holy Spirit convicts our hearts of the areas that need to be dealt with — areas where we need to repent of wrong and surrender something to Him. When we repent, the blockages are removed, and often the answers come quickly.

Friend, God is a wonderful Father and He loves you. Yet, while He wants to give you your heart's desires, He also wants you to give Him your heart. For it is from your heart that all the issues of life flow (*see* Proverbs 4:23).

Remember, we didn't choose God; He chose us (*see* John 15:16). We have been redeemed from the devil's dominion by the precious blood of Jesus, and we no longer belong to ourselves (*see* 1 Corinthians 6:19; 1 Peter 1:18,19). Our lives belong to Him, and sometimes He is waiting for us to surrender something to Him.

Hannah became willing to give up the one thing she wanted very badly — her son. When she did, she received the answer to her prayer and a bonus blessing of three more sons and two daughters! This demonstrates that God often wants to give us things, but He's waiting for us to hold things open-handedly and give Him ownership. He's waiting for surrender.

As You Continue in Prayer, 'Watch' and Be 'Thankful'

Along with continuing in prayer, we are also instructed to "…watch in the same with thanksgiving" (Colossians 4:2). The word "watch" here is a form of the marvelous Greek word *gregoreo*, which means *to be on your guard*, *to be watchful*, or *attentive*. It primarily denotes the watchful attitude of one who is on the lookout to make certain no enemy or aggressor can successfully gain entry into his life or place of residence.

Additionally, this word *gregoreo* means *to be on high alert*, and it depicts a person whose attitude is to never let up being watchful. Thus, to "watch" means *to be awake* or *to be alert*. One expositor has translated it, *"…Be wide awake…."* Rather than go to sleep on the job, you need to *keep your eyes wide open* so you can watch for the answer!

Unfortunately, many people go to sleep in prayer, which is like going to sleep on the job. That's what happened with the apostles the night when Jesus was betrayed in the Garden of Gethsemane. Instead of remaining watchful, they kept falling asleep on the job that Jesus asked them to do. Don't let that happen to you.

You need to stay *wide awake* and to stay alert!

Remember, you are supposed to be *pressing into the Spirit* and *committed to not give up until you have obtained what you are praying for*. Of course, as you are continuing in prayer, you may become "weary." That's why Paul says, "Watch!" It is like the Holy Spirit is saying, *"Stay awake! Stay on your guard! Keep your eyes open!"* Why? Because the answer is on the way, and you don't want to miss it.

While you watch, offer God *thanksgiving*. The Greek word for "thanksgiving" used here in Colossians 4:2 is *eucharistia*, and it depicts *an outpouring of heart full of grace* and *feelings that freely flow from the heart in response to someone or something*.

This free-flowing heart of thanksgiving is *the voice of faith*! It takes faith to thank God for something we haven't seen yet. Thanking God for what He is going to do and going to provide *before* it is received is evidence of faith. We see an example of this in John 11:41 when Jesus stood in front of Lazarus' tomb while he was still dead and prayed, "…Father, I thank thee that thou hast heard me." It was *after* Jesus thanked God that, "…He cried with a loud voice, Lazarus, come forth" (John 11:43).

Friend, when you're in a position of thanksgiving, you're not in doubt or unbelief and you're not murmuring or complaining. You are in a position of faith, and when God hears your thanksgiving and sees your faith, He is drawn to you. Like the sweet smell of savory food being cooked in the kitchen, your thanksgiving (*eucharistia*) attracts God's presence to you. And when He comes, He brings the full weight of His glory with Him, which includes the answers to your prayers. Never underestimate the power of thanksgiving!

So what should you do if you are praying in faith and the answer still hasn't come? You need to "continue in prayer," which means *keep pressing* in the Spirit toward the answer. Be willing to make whatever changes God may require of you and keep your eyes open for the answer. Finally, lift your voice, and start thanking God for the answer even *before* it comes!

STUDY QUESTIONS

> Study to shew thyself approved unto God, a workman that needeth not to be ashamed, rightly dividing the word of truth.
> — 2 Timothy 2:15

1. The biggest obstacle you need to press through every day is your *flesh*. The Bible says, "...The mind of the flesh [which is sense and reason without the Holy Spirit] is death [death that comprises all the miseries arising from sin, both here and hereafter]..." (Romans 8:6 *AMPC*). What does God say about the flesh? Here are some things you really need to know:

   - Romans 7:18 says _____ dwells in my flesh.
   - In John 6:63, Jesus said my flesh _____.
   - Romans 8:8,13 says if I live by my flesh _____.
   - Romans 13:14 instructs me not to _____.

2. The proven solution for dealing with the flesh is to *follow the leading of the Holy Spirit* (*see* Romans 8:1-17). The Bible says, "...The mind of the [Holy] Spirit is life and [soul] peace [both now and forever]" (Romans 8:6 *AMPC*). To help you understand the importance and power of following the Holy Spirit, here are some things you really need to know:

   - Galatians 5:16 declares if I follow the Sprit _____.
   - In John 16:13, Jesus said the Spirit will _____.
   - In John 14:26, Jesus said the Spirit will _____.
   - Galatians 5:22-25 says if I stay in step with the Spirit, these are the kind of things I can expect in my life: _____.

PRACTICAL APPLICATION

> But be ye doers of the word, and not hearers only, deceiving your own selves.
> —James 1:22

1. As you continue to press in, God is wanting you to come to a place of prayer where you say, "All right, Lord, is there anything in me that's stopping me from receiving from You? If so, what is it? What do I need to give up, place in Your hands, and walk away from so I can receive from You?" Be still and listen. What is the Holy Spirit speaking to your heart? If you don't hear a response immediately, be

at peace and keep your spiritual ears open during the days and weeks ahead. He will likely answer you when you least expect it.

2. Being "watchful" as you continue in prayer means being *wide awake and expecting* God to show up! Carefully meditate on Isaiah 30:18 (*AMPC*), which helps convey the importance of expectancy:

> And therefore the Lord [earnestly] waits [expecting, looking, and longing] to be gracious to you; and therefore He lifts Himself up, that He may have mercy on you and show loving-kindness to you. For the Lord is a God of justice. Blessed (happy, fortunate, to be envied) are all those who [earnestly] wait for Him, who expect and look and long for Him [for His victory, His favor, His love, His peace, His joy, and His matchless, unbroken companionship]!

What does this passage say to you about *God's expectancy* and *your expectancy*? Why is it vital for you to have a heart of expectancy as you pray and wait on the Lord? What are you expecting from Him?

LESSON 10

TOPIC

What To Do if Answers to Your Prayers Are Delayed or Hindered, Part 2

SCRIPTURES

Philippians 4:6,7 — Be careful for nothing; but in every thing by prayer and supplication with thanksgiving let your requests be made known unto God. And the peace of God, which passeth all understanding, shall keep your hearts and minds through Christ Jesus.

GREEK WORDS

1. "careful" — μεριμνάω (*merimnao*): denotes anxiety, care, concern, or worry, or pictures a person who is deeply troubled; pictures a person

who is distracted or worrying about how his basic physical needs will be met

2. "nothing" — **μηδέν** (*meden*): absolutely nothing at all
3. "every thing" — **ἐν παντὶ** (*en panti*): in everything — and that means in every little detail
4. "prayer" — **προσευχή** (*proseuche*): close, up-front, intimate contact; coming close to express a wish, desire, prayer, or vow; originally used to depict a person who vowed to give something of great value to God in exchange for a favorable answer to prayer; portrays an individual who desires to see his prayer answered so desperately that he is willing to surrender everything he owns in exchange for answered prayer; contained in this word is the concept of surrender
5. "supplication" — **δέησις** (*deesis*): a request for a concrete, specific need — usually some type of physical or material need — to be met; a request for a physical, tangible need to be met or supplied; a petition
6. "thanksgiving" — **εὐχαριστία** (*eucharistia*): an outpouring of a heart full of grace, gratitude, and feelings that freely flow from the heart in response to someone or something
7. "requests" — **τὰ αἰτήματα** (*ta aitemata*): plural, petitions
8. "made known" — **γνωρίζω** (*gnoridzo*): to declare, to make known, or to broadcast
9. "peace" — **εἰρήνη** (*eirene*): the cessation of war; conflict put away; a time of rebuilding and reconstruction after war has ceased; distractions removed; a time of prosperity; the rule of order in the place of chaos; it is a calm, inner stability that results in the ability to conduct oneself peacefully even in the midst of circumstances that would normally be traumatic or upsetting; it is the Greek equivalent of the Hebrew word shalom, which expresses the idea of wholeness, completeness, or tranquility in the soul that is unaffected by outward circumstances or pressures
10. "passeth" — **ὑπερέχω** (*huperecho*): to be above, beyond, superior, or surpassing
11. "understanding" — **νοῦν** (*noun*): the mind, or comprehension and understanding
12. "keep" — **φρουρέω** (*phroureo*): a military term that expresses the idea of soldiers who stood faithfully at their post at the city gates to guard and control all who went in and out of the city; soldiers who served as

gate monitors and whose approval was necessary for anyone to enter the city

SYNOPSIS

David was a man after God's own heart, and in writing about the Lord's goodness, he declared, "The eyes of the Lord are upon the righteous, and his ears are open unto their cry. The righteous cry, and the Lord heareth, and delivereth them out of all their troubles" (Psalm 34:15,17). There is nothing more rewarding than for God to hear and answer us when we pray!

However, there are times when we pray and it seems like the heavens are made of brass, and nothing is getting through. What causes these hindrances and delays in our prayers from being answered? Here, once more, is a rundown of eight factors that influence and affect our prayers:

1. Praying inconsistently.
2. Praying incorrectly.
3. A lack of faith.
4. A negative confession.
5. Bad relationships.
6. Spiritual opposition.
7. Timing.
8. Sin.

Now, if you're doing everything you know to do to address these key issues, and you're still not getting answers to your prayers, God says you are to "continue in prayer, and watch in the same with thanksgiving" (Colossians 4:2). Essentially, this means you are to keep pressing through any obstacles and press into the Holy Spirit, God's Word, and prayer until you finally receive what you have been after.

The emphasis of this lesson:

God commands us not to worry or be anxious about anything but to bring Him all our specific needs in prayer, thanking Him in advance for the answers He will provide. This will cause His peace to act like a military guard that blocks the entrance to all foul emotions from entering our heart and mind.

Don't Worry or Be Anxious About Anything

"Well, what about worry and anxiety?" you might ask. "How are we supposed to respond to things when we have prayed and prayed, and nothing has changed? How are we to navigate the weight of worry and anxiety?"

To answer this question, we turn our eyes to what Paul wrote to the believers at the church in Philippi. He said,

> **Be careful for nothing; but in every thing by prayer and supplication with thanksgiving let your requests be made known unto God.**
>
> **And the peace of God, which passeth all understanding, shall keep your hearts and minds through Christ Jesus.**
> **— Philippians 4:6,7**

There are several important words in this passage, including the word "careful." This is a translation of the Greek word *merimnao*, and it denotes *anxiety*, *care*, *concern*, or *worry*. It is the picture of a person who is deeply troubled or one who is distracted or worrying about how his basic, physical needs will be met.

So, when the Bible says, "Be careful for nothing," God is telling us that there is nothing we are to have anxiety, care, concern, or worry about — *nothing*. And that word "nothing" is the Greek word *meden*, which means *absolutely nothing at all*.

Letting Go of Worry Is Something All of Us Must Learn

If you have been saved for a little while, you've probably heard messages taught on Philippians 4:6,7. Rick had certainly had his fill of teaching on this passage — so much so that he grew to despise it, because he worried about everything.

To make matters worse, he had been raised in a spiritual environment where they overused the word *burden*. For instance, everyone in his church was taught to say things like, "We have a burden for souls," and "We have a burden to pray." It seemed like having a burden was a badge of courage that everyone was taught to wear. Consequently, Rick grew up thinking that those who were spiritually mature were always to be burdened (concerned or worried) about something.

But that is not biblical. We're not supposed to carry our burdens. Instead, we are to cast our burdens on Jesus because He wants to be our beast of burden and carry them for us (*see* 1 Peter 5:7).

The fact that Rick was always eaten up with worry made Philippians 4:6 and 7 a passage he just couldn't understand. Even after he married his wife, Denise, he continued to be plagued with worry. In their early years together, when they would schedule a day to just have fun, Rick would start out enjoying himself, but eventually he would begin to think, *How can I be so unspiritual and irresponsible? I've not been burdened with anything today. What is wrong with me?* He would then move back into the mode of worry and being burdened.

Eventually, God enabled Rick to understand and come to grips with these verses and obey them. Through it all, he learned that worry is a choice. It is a decision of the will and the mind to work feverishly to try and figure everything out. Left unchecked, worry becomes a life-draining habit that can land you in the hospital. Just ask Rick. Worry was so out of control at one point in his life that he ended up needing a blood transfusion because he was bleeding internally from ulcers caused by constant worry.

Once Rick learned the meaning of Philippians 4:6 and 7, he repented of worry and walked away from it. That is what true repentance is — a decision of the mind to change direction. Rick turned away from worry and learned to trust God, which is what we can learn to do too.

We Are To Pray About 'Everything' and Bring God Specific Requests

Looking again at Philippians 4:6, it says, "Be careful for nothing; but in every thing by prayer and supplication with thanksgiving let your requests be made known unto God." So, God instructs us NOT to worry or be anxious about anything at all. Instead, He says pray about *everything*! The word "every thing" here is a translation of the Greek words *en panti*, which means *in everything* — and that indicates *in every little detail*.

You are to take every little detail of your life and "…by prayer and supplication with thanksgiving let your requests be made known unto God" (Philippians 4:6). The word "prayer" here is a form of the Greek word *proseuche*, the same word we saw in Colossians 4:2. It describes *close, up-front, intimate contact*. It is the picture of a person coming close to express a wish, desire, prayer, or vow.

Originally, this word *proseuche* was used to depict a person who vowed to give something of great value to God in exchange for a favorable answer to prayer. Here, it portrays an individual who desires to see his prayer answered so desperately that he is willing to surrender everything he owns in exchange for answered prayer. Thus, the word "prayer" describes *a place of exchange* and carries the concept of *surrender*.

Coupled with prayer, we see the word "supplication," which is a form of the Greek word *deesis*. This is *a request for a concrete, specific need — usually some type of physical, tangible, or material need — to be met or supplied*. The word *deesis* can also be translated as *a petition*, which is *a clear, well-stated request*.

Oftentimes, when we pray, God has no idea what we're asking for, because we verbalize our emotions. We pray inconsistently, asking for one thing and then changing it to something different. A petition, on the other hand, is a well-stated request. When we come to God, we need to bring a clear, concrete petition. It needs to be so exact and specific that when He answers, it will be a specific answer to what we have asked. That is what this verse says.

If you think about it, worry is so habitual it is unending. Once you finish worrying about one thing, you quickly move in to worrying about something else. Hence, worry becomes like an undertow in the ocean that grabs you and drags you back out to sea. A person who worries all the time wants to be in control of their circumstances, and somehow, they mistakenly feel that by worrying, they are in control.

The only way to end this vicious cycle of madness is to begin bringing every little detail of our life to God in prayer (*proseuche*) and surrender it to Him. In this place of exchange, we willingly give up control of our life and choose to trust God with every part of it. We say, "Jesus, You are Lord. You are the Supreme Master who is in charge and calling the shots — not me. I choose to surrender all my anxiety, my worry, and my fretting to you in exchange for Your priceless peace. I receive it now by faith, in Jesus' name. Amen."

We Are To Always Couple Our Requests With 'Thanksgiving'

Now, when we come to the altar of prayer with our specific, concrete petitions, Philippians 4:6 says we are to come with *thanksgiving*. This word "thanksgiving" is a form of the Greek word *eucharistia*, which is the same word we saw in Colossians 4:2. Again, it describes *an outpouring of a heart full of grace, gratitude,* and *feelings that freely flow from the heart in response to someone or something.* It is *the voice of faith.*

The use of this word *eucharistia* ("thanksgiving") tells us that as we are bringing our prayer petitions to God, we are also bringing Him thanks and expressing gratefulness for what He has already done. In other words, we're saying, "Father, thank You that You have heard me and that Your answer is already on the way. I worship You and thank You for Your kindness, mercy, and generous response to my request, in Jesus' name!"

This brings us to the word "requests," which in Greek is the plural form for *petitions*. Our petitions — our specific, clearly-stated requests — are to be "made known" to God. The words "made known" are a translation of the Greek word *gnoridzo*, which means *to declare, to make known,* or *to broadcast*. Hence, we are to clearly communicate our requests to Heaven like a broadcast. So not only does God hear you, but also all of Heaven — including the angels — hears you.

So, when Philippians 4:6 says, "Be careful for nothing; but in every thing by prayer and supplication with thanksgiving let your requests be made known unto God," it is saying:

- Don't worry or be anxious or fretful about anything.
- Bring God absolutely every little detail of your life that concerns you.
- Come to the place of surrender and exchange — that's prayer.
- Be very specific and clear in what you ask God to do.
- Bring Him all your multiple requests coupled with thanksgiving and gratefulness.
- Broadcast them confidently and clearly to God and all of Heaven.

What will happen when you choose to obediently follow these divine directions? The answer is unveiled in Philippians 4:7: "And the peace of

God, which passeth all understanding, shall keep your hearts and minds through Christ Jesus."

God's 'Peace' Will 'Keep' Our Heart and Mind

Notice the word "peace" in verse 7. It is the extraordinary Greek word *eirene*, which is the Greek equivalent of the Hebrew word *shalom*. It describes *the cessation of war* and *conflict being put away*. It pictures *a time of rebuilding and reconstruction after war has ceased*. All distractions are removed, and a time of prosperity comes.

Moreover, this word *eirene* — translated here as "peace" — depicts the rule of order in the place of chaos. It is a calm, inner stability that results in the ability to conduct oneself peacefully even in the midst of circumstances that would normally be traumatic or upsetting. And since it is the Greek equivalent of the Hebrew word *shalom*, it expresses the idea of *wholeness, completeness*, or *tranquility in the soul that is unaffected by outward circumstances or pressures*.

Friend, if you will obey God's command to bring all your cares and concerns to Him in prayer and communicate your specific requests with thanksgiving, you can become an island of peace even in the midst of traumatic circumstances.

The peace God gives is not the kind of peace the world gives. God's peace "passeth all understanding." The word "passeth" is a form of the Greek word *huperecho*, and it means *to be above, beyond, superior*, or *surpassing*. The Greek word for "understanding" here is a noun describing *the mind* or *comprehension and understanding*.

The Bible says that God's superior and surpassing form of peace is able to "keep" you, and this word "keep" is a translation of the marvelous Greek word *phroureo*. It is a military term and expresses the idea of soldiers who stood faithfully at their post at the city gates to guard and control all who went in and out of the city. These soldiers served as gate monitors, and their approval was necessary for anyone to enter the city.

By using this word "keep" (*phroureo*), God is telling us that His peace will stand at the gates of your heart, and if anything upsetting, peace-stealing, or worry-inducing tries to enter, the peace of God will deny it entrance just like the guards in the ancient cities. They would come together and cross their spears, forming an X and forbidding people entrance to the city.

Thus, the peace of God will block the entrance to all those foul emotions from getting into your heart and mind. It will literally *keep*, *protect*, and *monitor* your heart and mind so that they are not penetrated by worry, anxiety, or fear.

When we factor in the original Greek meaning of the key words in this verse, this is how the *Renner Interpretive Version* (*RIV*) of Philippians 4:7 reads:

> **And the peace of God — a peace that brings cessation to war, that puts conflict away, that ushers in a time of rebuilding and reconstruction, that removes distractions resulting in a time of prosperity, and that brings the rule of order in the place of chaos — I'm talking about a calm, inner stability that results in the ability to conduct yourself peacefully even in the midst of outward circumstances or pressures that would normally be traumatic or upsetting — a peace that cannot be compared to any other type of peace and that stands in a category by itself, far surpassing and going beyond anything the human mind could ever think, reason, imagine, or produce by itself — that very peace will stand at the entrance of your heart and mind, working like a guard to control, monitor, and screen everything that tries to access your mind, heart, and emotions**

Could you use this kind of peace in your life? Just imagine! God's superior peace working in your relationships. That means where you've had war and continual conflict, God's peace will bring about a cessation to war and put away conflict, ushering in a time of reconstruction. Rather than focusing on the fight, the peace of God will enable you to begin to rebuild things again. This supernatural peace is available to you every moment of every day, and the way to receive it is to not worry about anything but pray about everything.

Humble Yourself and Pray and God Will Answer

Friend, if you've been praying and praying and praying and you haven't received your answer yet, the enemy will tempt you to worry about things, but your worrying will only produce more anxiety, not peace. Your job is to follow God's instruction in Philippians 4:6: (bold removed)

> **Be careful for nothing; but in every thing by prayer and supplication with thanksgiving let your requests be made known unto God.**

If you will do verse 6, God will faithfully do verse 7:

> **And the peace of God, which passeth all understanding, shall keep your hearts and minds through Christ Jesus.**
> — Philippians 4:7

So, what is stealing your peace? What situations are draining you of joy? Whatever you're worrying about is what you should be praying about. If you're all caught up in anxiety, worry, and fear, there is no room for God's peace, and His answers are blocked from getting through to you. Likewise, if you're worrying, you are trusting in yourself and your own ability to figure things out instead of trusting in God, and that is pride. The Bible says, "…God resists the proud, but gives grace to the humble" (1 Peter 5:5 *NKJV*).

If you will humble yourself and say, "Help me, Lord! I can't figure anything out on my own. I've tried, and it doesn't work. Forgive me for my pride. I am surrendering these situations to You along with every minute detail of my life. You are the only One who sees everything perfectly and has the answers I need. I'm looking to You to fix things. Please flood my heart and mind with Your peace. In Jesus' name. Amen!"

Remember, "Draw nigh to God, and he will draw nigh to you…" (James 4:8). That is His promise. If you will regularly come close to the Lord in prayer and cast all of your cares on Him — every little detail of your life — and thank Him in faith for the answer He is bringing, then His unsurpassed, extraordinary peace will flood your heart and mind and guard it from all worry and fear!

STUDY QUESTIONS

> Study to shew thyself approved unto God, a workman that needeth not to be ashamed, rightly dividing the word of truth.
> — 2 Timothy 2:15

1. God doesn't want you to have anxiety, care, concern, or worry about anything — especially your basic needs. Jesus makes this crystal clear in Matthew 6:25-34 and Luke 12:22-32. Carefully read what He said and jot down — and commit to memory — the verses that build your faith to trust God to provide for you and your family. What else is the

Holy Spirit showing you about trusting Him and not worrying about the bare necessities in life?

2. One of the most important passages in the entire Bible regarding the need to trust God and not worry is found in Proverbs 3:5-8. Look up this passage in a few different Bible versions and write out the translation that impacts you most. Commit these verses to memory and ask the Holy Spirit to give you a solid heart revelation of its meaning.

3. It is vital for you to know that you have access to God's presence anytime, anywhere. Take a few moments to look up these key verses regarding approaching God's throne in prayer:

   - What's the one thing that gives you the right to approach God? (*See* Hebrews 10:19.)

   - What does God want you to pray about? (*See* Hebrews 2:14-18; 4:16; and 1 Peter 5:7.)

   - How does God want you to approach Him? (*See* Hebrews 4:16; 10:22; and Ephesians 3:12.)

   - What attitude must you have to receive anything from God? (*See* James 4:6; 1 Peter 5:5,6.)

PRACTICAL APPLICATION

> But be ye doers of the word, and not hearers only,
> deceiving your own selves.
> —James 1:22

1. Rick grew up thinking that those who were spiritually mature were always to be burdened about something. How about you? Do you believe it is honorable or the "Christian thing" to always be worried or concerned about something? How is this lesson helping you see that casting your cares on God and trusting Him is what He really wants you to do?

2. Instead of being anxious and worrying, God says you are to *pray about everything* — which means absolutely everything. Be honest: Are there certain areas of your life that you don't bring to God in prayer? If so, what are they, and why do you not pray about them?

3. When the Bible says we are to pray and bring "supplications" to God, it means our prayer requests are to be *concrete*, *clear*, and *specific*. Can

you remember a time when you prayed very specifically, and God answered it? What was your request? How did His answer affect your faith? How does remembering times like these increase your faith to keep praying?

A Prayer To Receive Salvation

If you've never received Jesus as your Savior and Lord, now is the time for you to experience the new life Jesus wants to give you! To receive God's gift of salvation that can be obtained through Jesus alone, pray this prayer from your heart:

> *Jesus, I repent of my sin and receive You as my Savior and Lord. Wash away my sin with Your precious blood and make me completely new. I thank You that my sin is removed, and Satan no longer has any right to lay claim on me. Through Your empowering grace, I faithfully promise that I will serve You as my Lord for the rest of my life.*

If you just prayed this prayer of salvation, you are born again! You are a brand-new creation in Christ! Would you please let us know of your decision by going to **renner.org/salvation**? We would love to connect with you and pray for you as you begin your new life in Christ.

Scriptures for further study: John 3:16; John 14:6; Acts 4:12; Ephesians 1:7; Hebrews 10:19,20; 1 Peter 1:18,19; Romans 10:9,10; Colossians 1:13; 2 Corinthians 5:17; Romans 6:4; 1 Peter 1:3

Notes

CLAIM YOUR FREE RESOURCE!

As a way of introducing you further to the teaching ministry of Rick Renner, we would like to send you FREE of charge his teaching, "How To Receive a Miraculous Touch From God" on CD or as an MP3 download.

In His earthly ministry, Jesus commonly healed *all* who were sick of *all* their diseases. In this profound message, learn about the manifold dimensions of Christ's wisdom, goodness, power, and love toward all humanity who came to Him in faith with their needs.

☑ YES, I want to receive Rick Renner's monthly teaching letter!

Simply scan the QR code to claim this resource or go to:
renner.org/claim-your-free-offer

WITH US!

R renner.org

f facebook.com/rickrenner • facebook.com/rennerdenise

▶ youtube.com/rennerministries • youtube.com/deniserenner

📷 instagram.com/rickrrenner • instagram.com/rennerministries_
instagram.com/rennerdenise